Excel 97

Basic skills
A progressive course for users

Jim Muir

Senior Lecturer in Business Computing
at Bournemouth University

Letts
1997

Acknowledgments

The computer program Microsoft Excel is copyrighted by the Microsoft Corporation, all rights reserved. Screen displays from Microsoft Excel are reprinted with permission. Microsoft Excel, Excel 97 and Windows 95 are registered trademarks of the Microsoft Corporation.

A CIP record for this book is available from the British Library.

ISBN 1 85805 219 X

Copyright © Jim Muir, 1997
Reprinted 1999 twice, 2000

Editorial and production services by Genesys Editorial

Typeset by Barbara Linton, Letts Educational, London

Printed in Great Britain by Ashford Colour Press, Gosport

Contents

ABOUT THIS BOOK

A note on the new Basic Skills edition

Each new version of Excel includes more and more features; it is no longer feasible to do them justice in a single, budget-price volume. To keep the size and the cost of the publication within acceptable limits the best solution is to divide the material into 'Basic Skills' and 'Further Skills' books.

This will benefit new users of Excel by allowing space to cover the introductory and intermediate stages in more detail. By the same token experienced users of Excel can cover the more advanced material in greater detail.

Who should use this book?

This book is intended for any new user of Excel 97. It is equally suitable for students in a classroom, an open-learning workshop or studying at home. It assumes no previous experience of Excel or any other spreadsheet packages. It provides a thorough grounding in tasks such as creating simple spreadsheet models, amending them and displaying the results as graphs or charts. Some intermediate skills are also covered, e.g. using more complex functions and analysis tools, linking worksheets together and using simple tables and macros.

The material used in this book makes no assumptions about students' previous experience of either computing, business or financial accounting. Both the Excel skills and their business applications are explained in simple terms, and the author has avoided biasing the examples towards areas where specialised numeric or accountancy skills are required.

If you have completed this book and need to extend your Excel skills you will find that the companion volume *Excel 97 Further Skills* contains much useful material.

Structure

Excel features are introduced in the context of practical business activities and problems to be solved, for example, sales figures, budgets, stock movements, expenditure etc, with the opportunity for further practice and consolidation.

This material has been organised into 13 units, each taking about 1 hour to complete. Every unit has the following features.

■ Introductory material plus a list of the skills covered in the unit and the prior skills needed to tackle it successfully.

■ Activities for acquiring and practising the skills in the context of practical business problems.

- Excel screens to help you check your learning.
- Summaries of commands and functions.
- Solutions, where appropriate, in the appendix.

The units are designed to be worked through in sequence, as activities build on the skills acquired in earlier units, and may use spreadsheets/charts created in previous activities.

A note to lecturers and students

This learning material requires little if any input by lecturers and can therefore be used in programmes of independent learning. The complete course material (covering both the Basic Skills and Further Skills books) is also available as a photocopiable resource pack (call 0181 740 2266 for details of the cost and terms of an institutional site licence). A disk containing the work achieved at the end of units is available free of charge to lecturers using the book as a course text; please write to the publisher on college headed paper or telephone 0181-740 2266 for further details.

Conventions

Terminology

The terms 'DOS' and 'MS-DOS' are used interchangeably.

The terms 'PC', 'personal computer' and 'computer' are used interchangeably.

Typographical conventions

Menu items and dialog boxes are shows as: **File**

Buttons are shown as: **Save**

Keys on the keyboard are shown as: <u>*ctrl*</u> /<u>A</u>

Filenames are shown as: **SUMMARY 1**

Names of fields, reports and other items created by the user are shown as: **Members**

Typed text is shown as: *=B9+B11*

(Note that text can be typed in upper or lower case.)

Functions and macro statements are shown as *SUM( )*

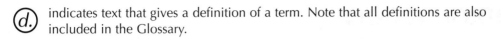 indicates text that gives a definition of a term. Note that all definitions are also included in the Glossary.

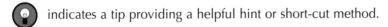 indicates a tip providing a helpful hint or short-cut method.

indicates a cautionary note.

indicates a cross reference.

indicates a feature that is new in Excel 97.

INTRODUCTION

Developments in Excel

Excel is produced by Microsoft Corporation, the US software company. It is specifically designed to operate using Windows, Microsoft's graphical operating environment.

Excel was first launched in 1987. The previous version, Excel 7, was introduced in 1995 specifically to operate with Windows 95.

Excel 97 was launched in January 1997 and, at the time of writing, is still operating under Windows 95. By the time you are using this book however, Excel may also be using Windows 97, the proposed update to Windows 95.

Earlier versions of both Excel and Windows are still widely used, especially in education. If you have used a previous version of Excel you will find that for standard operations the basic Excel menus, commands and screen layouts remain very similar and new features of later versions form natural add-ons.

What are spreadsheets?

Since the personal computer's initial impact on business in the 1980s, three types of business software have emerged as industry standards, the word-processor, the database management system and the spreadsheet. This is hardly surprising, as they fulfil three key business needs:

All businesses need to cope with the volumes of text that they create – letters, memos, reports, etc, – hence the word-processor.

They need to store and retrieve records of all types – stock, personnel, customer etc, – hence the need for database management systems.

Their third major need is handle numeric data – sales, profits, financial forecasts, stock movements and mathematical models of all kinds. The spreadsheet meets this need.

For many years businesses have used manual spreadsheets – large sheets of squared paper divided into columns and rows. Managers have used these sheets of paper 'spread out' on their desks to analyse various types of business information.

For example, it has been estimated that up to a third of a manager's time is typically spent preparing budgets. This involves such operations as manipulating, calculating and analysing numeric information, using formulae, inserting text and drawing graphs. When the data changes, lengthy and tedious recalculation becomes necessary.

A computer spreadsheet is simply the equivalent of this sheet of squared paper, with in-built calculating facilities.

A simple example of an Excel spreadsheet is shown below, calculating a student's personal finances; the columns represent the weeks, and the rows various categories of income and expenditure. The balance at week end is carried forward to the next week.

You could use this data in a variety of ways

- as a record of your past finances

- to budget for future expenditure

- to compare expenditure patterns week by week

- to experiment with the data to model possible increases in income or expenditure – what if rent rises by 10% in week 5?

- to draw graphs illustrating any of the above.

A	B	C	D	E	F
	PERSONAL FINANCES - TERM 1				
INCOME	Week 1	Week 2	Week 3	Week 4	Week 5
Opening Bals.	£0.00	£1,015.00	£885.00	£755.00	£625.00
Grant	£500.00				
Bank Loan	£400.00				
Parents	£300.00				
Total Income	£1,200.00	£1,015.00	£885.00	£755.00	£625.00
EXPENDITURE					
Accommodation	£60.00	£60.00	£60.00	£60.00	£60.00
Food and Travel	£30.00	£35.00	£35.00	£35.00	£35.00
Books	£75.00	£15.00	£15.00	£15.00	£15.00
Other	£20.00	£20.00	£20.00	£20.00	£20.00
Total Expenditure	£185.00	£130.00	£130.00	£130.00	£130.00
CLOSING BALS.	£1,015.00	£885.00	£755.00	£625.00	£495.00

Spreadsheet terminology

(d.) A spreadsheet is a grid of vertical *columns* and horizontal *rows*.

(d.) Where column and row intersect is a box or *cell*.

(d.) The cell reference or *address* consists of two co-ordinates – the column letter followed by the row number (as in a street map). Cells can contain text (labels) or numbers.

(d.) Certain cells can contain *formulae* which tell the spreadsheet to perform calculations, e.g. add a column or work out a percentage. These formulae ensure that totals are automatically recalculated when the values in the spreadsheet are changed.

(Excel use the term *worksheet* for their computer spreadsheet, this term will be used throughout this book.)

Advantages of spreadsheets

It is much easier to use a computerised spreadsheet, such as Excel, than to perform manual calculations. A spreadsheet is a general-purpose tool that can be used to solve a wide variety of problems – any information that can be represented as columns and rows. The advantages of spreadsheets should now be obvious.

- Reducing the drudgery of calculations.

- Reducing errors.

- Freeing user time to concentrate on problem solving.

- Allowing users to examine alternative solutions.

- Producing quicker results.

In the units that follow you will realise these advantages for yourself and gain an important business skill.

Jim Muir

July 1997

The Excel environment

What you will learn in this unit

By the end of this unit you will be able to

■ load and run Excel 97

■ use the mouse

■ understand the worksheet screen

■ create your own worksheet

■ use the Office assistant.

In this unit you'll learn such essential preliminaries as starting up the Excel package, using the mouse, and finding your way around the worksheet screen. Then you'll create your first worksheet and find out how to input and alter data. With a little practice, you will find them straightforward. Make sure that you read and follow the instructions in these activities carefully. You are bound to make a few mistakes at first – these are part of learning – but you will learn how to put them right for yourself.

Loading and running Excel

At the moment Excel 97 is a Windows 95 application. This means that Excel will not run unless the Windows 95 operating system is already loaded – up and running. By the time you use Excel 97 the later Windows version – Windows 97 – may be installed on your PC. This update will make little, if any difference to the start up instructions that follow. However, if your PC is using an earlier version of Windows, e.g. Windows 3.1 or Windows for Workgroups, then an earlier version of Excel, e.g. Excel 5 or earlier will be installed and you will need an earlier edition of this workbook.

Task 1: Loading Excel

There are different ways to load Excel, depending on how your computer has been set up. The following instructions will cover most situations.

First turn on your computer (and the screen too if necessary). If a screen appears that resembles FIGURE 1.1 below then Windows 95 has automatically loaded.

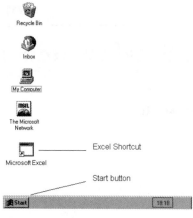

Recycle Bin

Inbox

My Computer

The Microsoft
Network

Microsoft Excel ——————— Excel Shortcut

Start button

Start   18:18

FIGURE 1.1

Look at FIGURE 1.1 carefully, it shows the Windows 95 *desktop* – the opening
screen from which all your Windows activities start. Your Windows 95 desktop may
look slightly different to this, depending on which options were installed. However
if it looks radically different, for example a Program Manager window has opened,
(perhaps overlaid by another window or so) then you have an earlier version of
Windows installed and therefore an earlier version of Excel than Excel 97 (see note
above).

On the desktop are various *icons* – small pictures of Windows 95 features.

At the bottom of the screen is the *Taskbar,* normally it shows just two objects, the
Start button on the left and the time on the right. However, as we will see later,
it also shows any tasks that are currently running, usually programs or applications
and any open files.

Use your desktop mouse to move the arrow-shaped pointer around the screen; this
is the *screen pointer* or *cursor.*

Starting Excel from a shortcut

Sometimes there is an Excel icon on the desktop, it will be labelled Excel 97, Office
97, Shortcut to Excel or similar (see FIGURE 1.1 above). You may need to look for it
carefully if there are a number of other icons. This shortcut will open Excel directly.
Move the screen pointer onto the Excel icon and click the left mouse button twice
in quick succession. Excel should start up now – if so go the section 'Excel users'
below.

Starting Excel from the Start menu

Move the screen pointer on top of the **Start** button and click the left button on
the mouse once.

A *pop-up* menu will open, move the mouse pointer onto the menu choice Programs
– a further menu opens – it will resemble FIGURE 1.2, depending on your computer
installation.

2

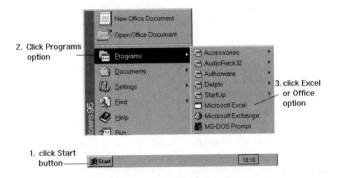

FIGURE 1.2

The next step will vary, depending on whether you have the whole Office 97 suite of programs installed, or only Excel 97.

Office 97 users

1   Move the mouse pointer onto the menu option Microsoft Office.

   A further menu window will open.

2   Move the mouse pointer onto the option Microsoft Excel.

3   Click the left mouse button once.

Excel users

1   Move the mouse pointer onto the menu option Microsoft Excel.

2   Click the left mouse button once.

Excel will begin to load (confirmed by an hour-glass symbol). For the first few seconds the Excel screen will be overlaid by an Excel 97 logo – use this to check the Excel version if necessary.

After a few seconds a blank Excel worksheet screen appears.

Task 2: Understanding the worksheet screen

A spreadsheet or *worksheet* is the computer equivalent of a large sheet of paper, divided into *columns* and *rows*. The columns and rows intersect to form rectangular cells where data is entered. A workbook consists of one or more *worksheets* – each worksheet can be regarded as a 'page' in the book. When you start Excel it opens a *Workbook window* – a group of related worksheets named initially Sheet1, Sheet2 etc. Look at the Excel screen below in FIGURE 1.3; it actually consists of two windows.

Around the outside is the *Application Window* that carries out all the Excel commands – menus, tool bars, etc.

Within the Application window is the *Document Window*. This consists of the worksheet itself, divided into columns and rows, plus other features such as scroll bars and sheet numbers.

Before we start using the keyboard or mouse let's identify the main components of the Excel screen. Keep referring to the labelled diagram below in FIGURE 1.3, *but don't use the keyboard or mouse yet.* Don't worry if your screen is slightly different, we're just identifying the main features at the moment.

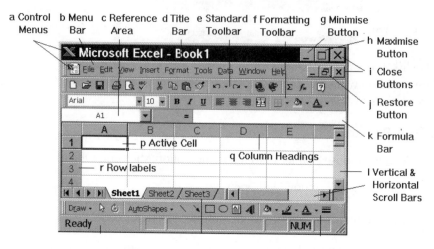

FIGURE 1.3

a. **The Control Menu Boxes**   We won't be using these features very much; they offer commands (e.g. re-sizing and closing the window) that can be better performed by other means.

b. **The Menu Bar**   The Menu Bar at the top of the screen shows a list of menu options – File, Edit, View, etc. The Excel commands are grouped under these menus.

c. **The Reference Area**   Shows the row and column number of the active cell – see p below.

d. **The Title Bar**   Whenever a new workbook is opened Excel gives it a temporary or default name, Book1, Book2 etc. This name will change when you save the workbook.

e. & f. **The Tool Bars**   There are two tool bars immediately below the menu bar; each bar consists of a row of buttons that you 'click' to carry out Excel tasks. Often a button is a shortcut alternative to a menu command, sometimes there is no menu alternative to using a button.

The Standard Toolbar   Offers options such as opening and closing files, cutting and pasting, printing, etc.

The Formatting Toolbar   Allows you to alter the appearance and alignment of data in your workbook.

In these units we concentrate mainly on the menu versions of commands, rather than using buttons. A key to these two tool bars is included at the end of this unit.

g – j.   At the top right of the screen are 2 groups of 3 buttons; these control the size of the worksheet screen. One set is for the whole application window and one for the inner cell area – the document window.

g. **The Minimize Button** (a line)   Reduces the size of the screen to a small icon.

h. **The Maximize Button** (a square)   Increases the window to fill the screen.

i. **The Close Button** (an 'X')   Closes the workbook. If you click this button by mistake then you will need to open Excel again.

j. **The Restore Button** (overlapping squares)   Restores the window to its original size.

k. **The Formula Bar**   Shows whatever is in entered in the active cell – see point p below. This is a new workbook so all the cells are blank.

l. **The Vertical and Horizontal Scroll Bars**   Allow you to move around a worksheet. The present worksheet window can only show a small fraction of the total worksheet size; potentially each sheet in a workbook can be 256 columns across and 65,536 rows down.

m.**The Drawing Toolbar**   Allows you to draw a variety of shapes on your worksheet – circle, rectangle, arrow etc. It also allows you to add colour and text effects. A key to this Toolbar is included at the end of this unit.

n. **Sheet Names**   A new workbook consists of a number of blank worksheets, having the default names Sheet1, Sheet2 etc. Collectively these form a workbook. Each sheet is marked with a name *tab* – the name in bold indicates which sheet is currently selected or 'active'.

o. **The Status Bar**   Displays information about the current command; no command has been issued yet so it reads 'Ready'.

p. **The Active Cell**   At the moment the top left cell A1 is the active cell – the one currently selected and shown by a heavy border. As we will see later, you cannot enter information into a cell unless it has first been selected and made 'active'. In Excel 97 a cell can contain up to 32,000 characters.

q. **Column Headings** and r, **The Row Headings**   These contain the column references (letters) and the row references (numbers). Jointly they give the cell *reference* or *address*, e.g. A1, D5.

Now that we've identified the basic screen components let's try some of them out; keep referring to FIGURE 1.3 if necessary. First we will experiment with the window size; this often causes problems when you're starting out.

Task 3: Minimising the window size

As explained in Task 2 above there are two windows in the Excel screen; each of these can be re-sized independently of the other window.

1   Move the screen pointer onto the topmost **Minimize** button at the top right of the screen. It is marked with a single line.

2   Click the left mouse button once. The whole workbook disappears, and you return to Windows.

On the Taskbar at the bottom of the screen is a button marked
Microsoft Excel – Book1 ; this represents the minimised worksheet – the Excel application is still running, but cannot be used until it is restored to normal size – see FIGURE 1.4.

3   Move the screen pointer onto this button and click the left mouse button once. The Excel window reappears – try again if it doesn't.

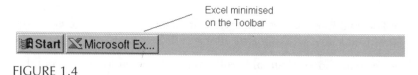

Excel minimised
on the Toolbar

FIGURE 1.4

Troubleshooting

- If you can't locate the Excel icon hold down the *Alt* key on the keyboard then press the *Tab* key. This key is on the left of the keyboard and marked with two opposite-facing arrows.

- Continue to keep *Alt* pressed down and press the *Tab* key. Windows runs through all your open applications until it finds Excel.

- At this point release the *Tab* then the *Alt* key. You are returned to Excel.

Task 4: Maximising and restoring the window size

1   Check whether there are two sets of **Maximize/Minimize/Close** buttons.

If so, the top set of buttons is for the Application Window and the set below for the Document Window – see FIGURE 1.5.

2   Click the topmost **Maximize** button. The Excel window fills the whole screen.

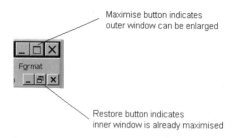

Maximise button indicates
outer window can be enlarged

Restore button indicates
inner window is already maximised

FIGURE 1.5

If the **Restore** button is displayed in the top set of buttons rather than the **Maximize** button then click it with the left mouse button (see FIGURE 1.5) – the window reverts to its previous size.

3 If there is a second `Restore` button below the top set of buttons on your worksheet then click it. This restores the size of the document window and makes two other changes.

The document window gets its own Title Bar – 'Book1'.

The `Restore` button changes to a `Maximize` button.

Try these procedures again until you get the hang of them – remember that:

if the `Maximize` button is displayed then the Window can be *maximised*.

if the `Restore` button is displayed then the Window is already maximised and can be restored to whatever size it was previously.

4 Click the `Minimize` button for the *document* window, i.e. the lower of the two sets of buttons. The outer Application window is not affected, but the inner Document window is shrunk to an icon – see FIGURE 1.6.

Click the `Restore` button on this icon to restore it.

FIGURE 1.6

Task 5: Adjusting window size

It is also possible to alter the size of the workbook window by 'dragging' the sides.

1 Move the screen pointer to the bottom right-hand edge of the inner document window – see FIGURE 1.7. The screen pointer changes to a double-headed arrow when correctly located.

If you cannot find the edge of the window then click the `Maximize` or `Restore` button on the document window (lower of the two sets of buttons).

locate screen pointer on the
bottom left-hand corner of window

FIGURE 1.7

2 Now press down the left mouse button and keep it pressed down.

3 Drag the edge of the worksheet diagonally towards the top left of the screen until you have reached cell D8. Then let go. Your document window should now look like FIGURE 1.8.

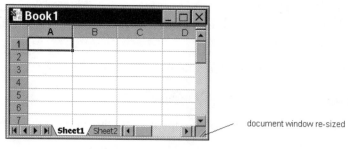

document window re-sized

FIGURE 1.8

4   Similarly drag the bottom right-hand edge of the application window so that it fits closely around the document window – see FIGURE 1.9. If you can't see the sides then you may need to click the **Restore** button first.

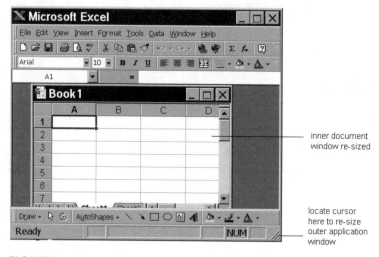

inner document window re-sized

locate cursor here to re-size outer application window

FIGURE 1.9

5   Restore both windows to a workable size by reversing this dragging process. Notice that the sides of a window can also be dragged in order to adjust the window size vertically or horizontally.

Task 6: Moving a window

First make sure that neither the application window nor the document window are maximised – click the **Restore** buttons if they are.

1   Move the pointer onto the Title Bar of the Application Window. It should read 'Microsoft Excel'.

2   Press down the left mouse button then drag the mouse – the whole window can be moved. This is useful if part of the window is off-screen.

If the document window is currently displaying its own title bar – it should read 'Book1'. Try moving this too. Moving the windows around may mean that the scroll bars are hidden. Restore the application and document windows if this happens.

Mouse control

You have now learnt two basic mouse actions.

■ **Clicking:** locate screen pointer, press left mouse button once

■ **Dragging:** locate screen pointer, hold down left button while moving mouse, release button.

You will soon be learning two further actions:

■ **Double clicking:** locate screen pointer and press mouse button twice in quick succession.

■ **Right clicking:** locate screen pointer, press right mouse button once.

From now on these terms will be used to refer to these actions.

Task 7: Scrolling around the screen

There are four ways to change the part of the worksheet window currently being displayed on screen. Try these, using FIGURE 1.10 below as a reference.

1 Move your pointer to the **vertical scroll bar** and locate it on the **down arrow** button.

2 Click once. The worksheet scrolls up a few rows. Notice the row numbers change – row 1 is no longer the top row.

3 Hold the mouse button down on the **down arrow** button. The rows scroll continuously.

4 Use the **up arrow** button to reverse the scrolling. Row 1 will eventually move to the top of the window again.

5 Now move the pointer near the bottom of the vertical scroll bar (not on the arrow button) and click. The rows scroll down, a screenful at a time.

6 Now identify the rectangular *scroll box* on the vertical scroll bar. Try dragging this box – it will scroll the worksheet more quickly.

   Notice that a **scroll tip** box indicates the row that you are moving to.

Repeat these operations for the *horizontal scroll bar* which controls the columns.

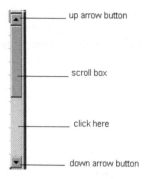

FIGURE 1.10

Task 8: Keyboard commands

Let's try out some keyboard commands which also change the screen position.

1   Hold down the *Ctrl* key and press the *Home* key. You are returned to the top of the worksheet – cell A1 is the active cell.

2   Hold down the *Ctrl* key and press the *down arrow* key on the keyboard. You are taken to the last row of the worksheet. (If the worksheet is not empty you are moved to the last row containing an entry.)

3   Now hold down the *Ctrl* key and press the *right arrow* key. You are taken to the last column of the worksheet.

Now try out the key combinations:

Ctrl – left arrow

Ctrl – up arrow

You will return to the top of the worksheet again.

The *Page up* and *Page down* keys can also be used.

 These keys are vital – not only in moving to cells, but also in finding your way back to the correct part of the worksheet. You can avoid that lost panicky feeling when all your data seems to have disappeared. Usually it is out of view in another part of the worksheet!

Task 9: Selecting individual cells

1   Maximize the worksheet window.

2   Return to the top of the worksheet and click cell A2. You have just selected a cell, the **reference box** lists it, showing that it has become the active cell.

3   Now move the screen pointer to cell C3, using either the mouse or the arrow keys on the keyboard. This becomes the active cell.

4   Experiment a few more times and select cells H12, F18 and E14.

5   Now using the screen controls, select cells M84, HJ127 and E216 in turn.

Task 10: Selecting groups of cells

You can also select groups or *ranges* of cells and whole columns or rows.

1   Move to cell A1.

2   Hold down the left mouse button, and drag the screen pointer down and across to cell D6.

3   Release the mouse button. 24 cells should be selected in all – see FIGURE 1.11.

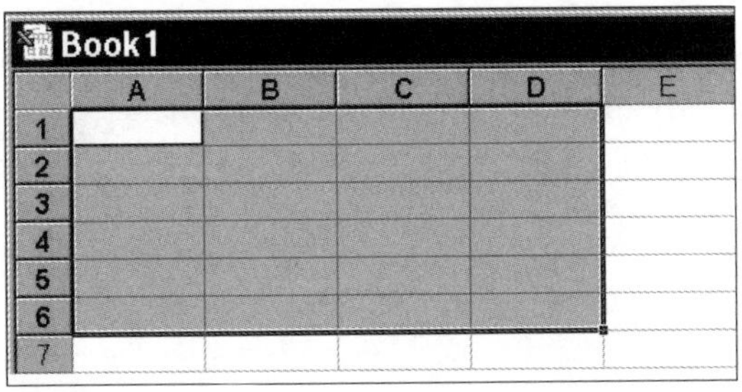

FIGURE 1.11

Notice that A1, the first cell selected, remains white while the others go dark. The cell and column labels (A – D and 1 – 6) are also shown in bold.

A1 remains the *active* cell in the range.

The cell *range* A1 to D6 is now selected.

Deselect this cell range by clicking anywhere on the worksheet.

Now try selecting a whole column – click on the column heading for column A (see FIGURE 1.12).

The column letter A is called the *column designator*. The whole column is selected.

5   Several columns can be selected by dragging across the column designators with the mouse pointer – try this for rows too.

 Selecting or 'highlighting' cells is an essential first step in many operations; it requires a little practice to select the precise range of cells.

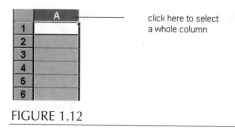

FIGURE 1.12

Task 11: Sheet names

Click on each sheet tab in turn – Sheet1, Sheet2 etc – to open a new sheet.

All the sheets are blank at the moment. The name in bold indicates which sheet is currently selected or 'active' (see FIGURE 1.13). You may have to re-size the document window if the sheet names are not in view – see Task 5 above.

On the left of the sheet names are a number of arrow buttons to move quickly through a group of worksheets. Try these out, finally selecting Sheet1.

FIGURE 1.13

Task 12: Menus

Now let's try selecting some commands from the *Menu Bar.* Menus are your major means of issuing commands. Choosing a command involves two steps:

■ opening the menu
■ selecting an option.

1   Move the screen pointer onto the Menu Bar at the top of the window.

2   Click the word **Edit**.

This opens the **Edit** menu and displays a *pull-down* menu of commands – see FIGURE 1.14. Edit is a typical menu – it contains a number of *options,* each of which executes a command.

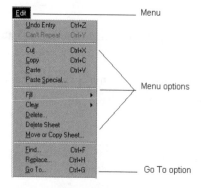

FIGURE 1.14

3   Click elsewhere on the worksheet and close the **Edit** menu.

4   Now open the **Edit** menu again; this time click the **Go To** option – see FIGURE 1.14 above.

A *dialog box* appears – see FIGURE 1.15.

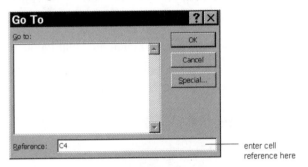

FIGURE 1.15

Task 13: Dialog Boxes

Dialog boxes are used when you need to enter some further information about the option that you have chosen. Sometimes this information is entered by clicking a button, sometimes by entering information from the keyboard. Standard dialog box buttons are

■ **Cancel**   Cancel Command

■ **OK**   Execute Command

■ **Help**   Seek help on command.

1   Enter the cell reference C4 in the Reference box, as shown in FIGURE 1.15 above. You may need to click the reference section of the dialog box first to locate the cursor there.

2   Click the **OK** button. The **Go To** option goes to the named cell (C4) and activates it.

Task 14: Shortcut keys

Some Excel users (usually proficient typists) may prefer to issue commands from the keyboard, rather than using the mouse and pull-down menus. You will notice that each menu title on the Menu Bar has one of its letters underlined, Eile, Edit, View etc.

1   Hold down the *Alt* key then type the appropriate letter, e.g. hold down the *Alt* key and type *F*.

The menu selection will be displayed.

2   Press the *Alt* or the *F10* key to close the menu.

13

There are similar shortcuts for the menu selections themselves, and many other Excel features. In these units we shall use the mouse rather than the keyboard to issue commands.

Task 15: Calling up Help

Excel provides a comprehensive online help and tutorial facility. You call **Help** by using the **Help** menu.

1 Move the screen pointer onto the Menu Bar and click the Help menu – see FIGURE 1.16.

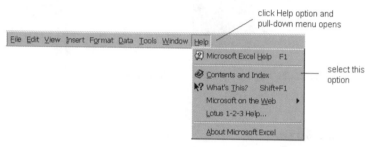

FIGURE 1.16

2 Select the second menu option **Contents** and **Index**. A dialog box opens.

3 Look at the top left hand corner of the dialog box. Three choices are shown as tabs: Contents, Index, Find (see FIGURE 1.17). Tabs are a common dialog box feature. Click the **Contents** and the **Index** tabs in turn and a new dialog box appears. If you click the **Find** tab then you should click the **Cancel** button

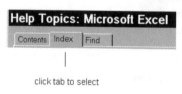

FIGURE 1.17

Task 16: Help Contents

1 Click the **Contents** tab.

The help contents are divided into topics, represented as chapters in a book.

2 *Double click* on the topic **Getting Help** (i.e. click the mouse button twice in quick succession).

The icon changes to an open book showing a series of subtopics – see FIGURE 1.18.

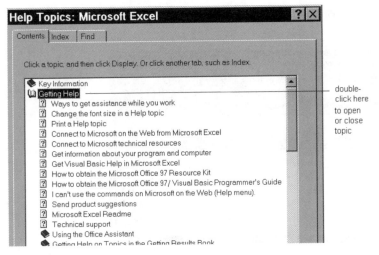

FIGURE 1.18

Read a few of these subtopics, (double click on them) returning to the **Contents** dialog box by clicking the **Back** or the **Help Topics** buttons.

3 Finally double-click the Getting Help topic to close it. The icon changes from an open to a closed book again.

Task 17: The Help Index

1 Click the **Index** tab at the top of the **Help** dialog box – see FIGURE 1.18 above if necessary.

All the Help topics are listed alphabetically. Provided you are fairly sure of your topic this feature can be easier to use than the Contents option which, as we have seen, involves negotiating several levels of contents.

2 Let's view the list of index topics and take this opportunity to try out different scrolling techniques – see FIGURE 1.19 for reference.

Scrolling techniques

Slow scrolling Position the mouse pointer on the up or down arrow and click once. The text scrolls a line at a time

Continuous scrolling Position the mouse pointer on the up or down arrow and keep the mouse button pressed down. The text scrolls continuously.

Rapid scrolling Identify the scroll box on the scroll bar – its position indicates your position in the list. Click above or below it and the topics move up in blocks.

3 Try dragging this box now; you can move to the start or end of the list quickly. Now scroll down to the topic **Menus – Customizing** and click it to select it- see FIGURE 1.19.

4 Click the **Display** button at the bottom of the dialog box and the help text is displayed.

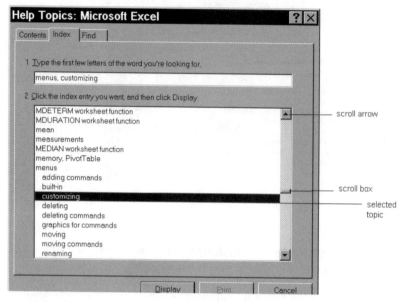

FIGURE 1.19

When you have read it click the **Help Topics** button to return to the dialog box.

Task 18: Keying in a Help topic

A quicker way than scrolling through a long list is to type in the name of the topic. The top part of the **Index** dialog box, labelled 1, allows you to do this – see FIGURE 1.20.

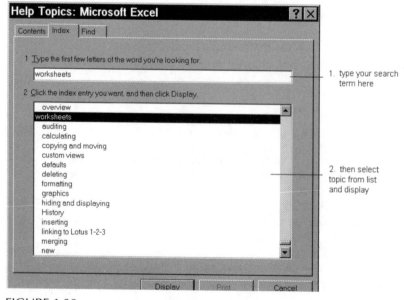

FIGURE 1.20

1   Move the mouse pointer to the start of the text in box 1. It should currently be empty; if not drag to highlight any text that it currently contains.

2   Now type in the new topic **worksheets.** The index moves to this section of topics.

3   Move the pointer to box number 2.

4   Scroll down to and then select the subtopic Worksheets – overview and display the help text as before. When you have read it click the **Help Topics** button to return to the dialog box.

Independent activity

Excel offers another way of getting help – Find. This is offered as a third tab option on the dialog box. Take some time to explore it.

Task 19: Exiting Help

Click either the **Close** or the **Cancel** button. You are returned to the workbook.

Task 20: Using the Office Assistant

The Office Assistant is new to Excel 97 and supplements other Help features by answering questions typed in ordinary English.

Look at the Standard Tool Bar at the top of the screen. The **Office Assistant** button is marked with a question mark – see the key to the Tool Bar at the end of this unit. If it is not in view then you may need to maximise the Application Window

1   Click the **Office Assistant** button once. The Office Assistant window opens, offering 4 options.

2   Let's try the first one 'What would you like to do?'

Using FIGURE 1.21 as a guide, first click on the text box.

3   Type **'close a window'** as shown.

4   Click the **Search** button.

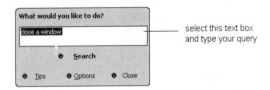

FIGURE 1.21

The Office Assistant displays a list of relevant topics – choose one by clicking it and the relevant help window appears. When you have read it close the window using the **Close** button at the top right of the window.

You are returned to Office Assistant logo – an animated paperclip. Click it once to display the Office Assistant window again.

This time click the **Tips** button – a screen tip appears. You can use the **Back** and **Next** buttons to display further tips when available.

Click the **Close** button on the Tips window. You are returned to the Office Assistant logo. Close it using the **Close** button.

Task 21: The 'What's This?' feature

This offers 'context sensitive' tips, i.e. specific to the Excel feature that you are currently using.

1 Open the **Help** menu.

2 Select the **What's This?** option.

3 Move the screen cursor around the window. Every time that it changes to a '?' shape you can click to get help on this feature.

4 Now move the screen pointer onto an Excel feature, e.g. open one of the menus and select an option. A ScreenTip window opens explaining its function. Simply click again to remove the screen tip. You can use ScreenTips whenever you're not sure what a particular Excel item does. To find out about another item you will need to open the **Help** menu and select the What's This? option again.

5 **Help on the Button Bars**   For a brief description of each button's purpose simply move the mouse pointer on top of it.

   For a more detailed description use the 'What's this?' option again.

Task 22: Exiting from Excel

1 Click the **File** option on the Menu Bar. The **File** menu opens.

2 Click the Exit option at the bottom of the menu and you leave Excel. As you have entered no data in the worksheet you should not be prompted to save it. If you are offered this option click the **No** button.

Summary of commands

Menu commands show the menu name first, followed by the command to choose from the menu, e.g. Edit-Clear means open the **Edit** menu and select the Clear command.

Keyboard commands use the dash symbol to indicate keys that should be pressed down at the same time, e.g. *Ctrl-Home*.

Keyboard Commands

Ctrl-Home	Go to cell A1
Ctrl-Down Arrow Key	Go to last row of the worksheet
Ctrl-Right Arrow Key	Go to last column of worksheet

Menu Commands

Edit-Go To	Go to specified cell
File-Exit	Exit Excel

Standard toolbar

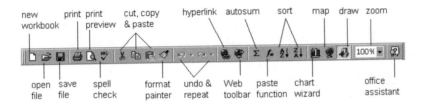

Formatting toolbar

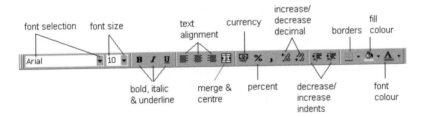

The drawing toolbar

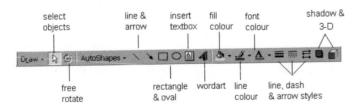

Summary of unit

In this unit you have learned how to

- load Excel and start it
- identify the main features of the worksheet screen
- maximise and minimise the window size
- adjust the window size
- control the mouse by dragging and clicking
- scroll around the screen
- select individual cells and groups of cells
- use sheet names, menu bars, dialog boxes and shortcut keys
- call up Help
- use the Office Assistant
- use the 'What's This?' feature
- exit from Excel.

Creating a worksheet

What you will learn in this unit

By the end of this unit you will be able to

- enter some simple data into a worksheet
- use formulae and functions to perform calculations
- delete, edit and copy data
- open and close an existing workbook.

What you should know already

Skill	Covered in
Identification of the basic elements of the Excel Window	Unit 1

Introduction

Now that we know our way around the Excel screen we can create our first worksheet. We'll choose a simple example – managing one's personal finances.

Look at FIGURE 2.1.

	A	B	C	D	E	F
1			PERSONAL FINANCES - TERM 1			
2	INCOME		Week 1			
3	Opening Bals					
4	Grant					
5	Loan					
6	Parents					
7	Total Income					
8						
9	EXPENDITURE					
10	Accomodation					
11	Food					
12	Books					
13	Other					
14	Total Expenditure					
15						

FIGURE 2.1

The worksheet is based around a student's income and expenditure for a term. Later on you can adapt it if you like to suit your own circumstances; for the moment enter the data exactly as shown here.

Entering data into a worksheet

 First enlarge the workbook windows if necessary by clicking the Maximize button (see Unit 1, 'Understanding the worksheet screen'). Make sure that **Sheet1** is the active sheet (click the sheet tab if necessary)

Task 1 Entering titles and labels

1 First click cell C1 to activate it. The reference C1 is now displayed in the reference area and the cell is outlined with a border.

2 Now enter the title shown in FIGURE 2.1 – ***PERSONAL FINANCES – TERM 1*** (simply start typing). Notice that the title displays in the Formula Bar as you type it – see FIGURE 2.2.

3 Press the ***Enter*** key. This large L-shaped key is located on the right of the keyboard and marked with a curled arrow. The title appears, displayed across several cells; this is as it should be.

We are now ready to enter the cell labels in column A. (A *label* is any text that labels or identifies cells.)

4 Activate cell A2 (i.e. click it) and enter the first label *INCOME*.

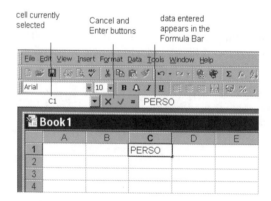

FIGURE 2.2

 Whenever you enter or change a cell's contents you need to complete the entry. There are several ways to do this:

■ press *Enter*

■ click the next cell

■ press one of the arrow keys on the keyboard

■ click the green 'tick' box that appears next to the Formula Bar (see FIGURE 2.2 above).

Text is automatically aligned to the left of the cell.

Forgetting to complete the entry causes a number of problems, e.g. menu options being dimmed and unavailable. Always check this if your next command fails to execute.

5   Carry on and complete all the labels in column 1, including the wrong spelling of the word 'Accomodation' .

    Don't worry if some labels overlap into the next column.

6   Enter the column heading for week 1 in cell **C2**.

Errors: Use the *Backspace* key (a large key at the top right of the keyboard, marked with a reverse arrow) to correct any errors that you notice while completing an entry. If you have finished entering the data then the Undo button on the Standard Toolbar will remove it (see key at the end of this unit).

Don't worry about errors that you notice at a later stage – we will correct them in later sections.

Task 2: Checking spelling

1   First click cell A1.

2   Move the screen pointer onto the Spelling button on the Standard toolbar.

    It is marked with a tick and 'ABC' – a small label appears to identify it – see FIGURE 2.3.

Spelling button

FIGURE 2.3

3   Click the Spelling button. Excel compares all the text in the selected cells with its dictionary. A dialog box opens, telling you, e.g., that the abbreviation 'Bals' is not in the dictionary.

4   Click the Ignore button.The label 'Accomodation' is selected; it has been misspelt with only one 'm'. Excel suggests the correct spelling.

5   Click the Change button.

6   Continue until a dialog box informs you that all the text is checked, then click the OK button.

Spell Checkers will not recognise most abbreviations and proper names, unless you add them to the dictionary. An `Add` button is provided to do this.

Task 3: AutoCorrect

1   Move the mouse pointer onto the word **Tools** on the menu bar – see FIGURE 2.4.

2   Select the option **AutoCorrect**, a dialog box appears. Commonly misspelt words and other common errors shown in the dialog box can be corrected as you type.

3   Click the `OK` button if you wish to use this feature.

    This feature can be turned off by selecting AutoCorrect again and then clicking the option box **'Replace text as you type'** to remove the 'X'.

FIGURE 2.4

Task 4: Editing cell contents using the formula bar

Let's alter the text in cell A5 from 'Loan' to 'Bank Loan'

1   Click cell A5 to activate it. The text appears in the Formula Bar at the top of the screen – see FIGURE 2.5.

2   Move the mouse pointer in front of the first letter of 'Loan' in the *Formula Bar* (not the cell). The pointer changes to a vertical bar.

3   Click *once* to place a flashing cursor there – this marks the *insertion point*.

4   Type the word 'Bank' and press *Enter*. The cell is amended.

locate cursor here
and click

	A	B	C
			PERSONA
1			
2	INCOME		Week1
3	Opening Bals		0
4	Grant		500
5	Loan		400
6	Parents		300
7	Total Income		1200
8			

FIGURE 2.5

Task 5: In-cell editing

You can also edit cell contents directly without using the Formula Bar. Let's alter the label 'Food' in cell A11 to 'Food and Travel'.

1 Move the screen pointer to cell **A11** and *double* click the space after the word 'Food'.

A flashing cursor marking the insertion point should be placed there – if not keep trying!

2 Amend the label to **'Food and Travel'** and press *Enter*.

Information only

Deleting If you need to delete any character, you must place the insertion point in the same way as above, then:

■ use the *Delete* key to delete to the right of the insertion point

■ use the *Backspace* key to delete to the left of the insertion point

■ relocate the pointer by clicking another cell.

Overtyping To overtype the contents of a cell, just click the cell once to select it and start typing. There is no need to delete the contents first.

Task 6: Widening columns

Some of the labels in Column A are too wide for their cells. Try out the three alternative methods that follow.

Method 1

1 Locate the screen pointer on the vertical line that separates column heading A from column heading B – see FIGURE 2.6. The pointer changes to a double-headed arrow.

2 Press down the left mouse button and drag the column to the *right* until its width is about 16.00. The width is given in the Reference Area.

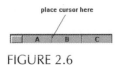

FIGURE 2.6

Method 2

1 Click the column designator, i.e. the 'A' in the column heading. The whole column is selected.

2 Click on the **Format** menu to open it.

3   Select the **Column** option then **Width** from the next menu that appears. A dialog box is displayed – see FIGURE 2.7 below.

4   Enter the new width as 15, and click the **OK** button.

Method 3

1   Click the column designator A again to select the column if necessary.

2   Open the **Format** menu and select the **Column** option then **AutoFit Selection**. The width is automatically adjusted to fit the longest entry.

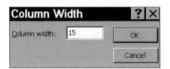

FIGURE 2.7

Task 7: Altering the row height

We will now make row 1 higher to emphasise the title.

1   Locate the screen pointer on the horizontal line that separates row designator 1 from row designator 2.

2   Drag the row down until the height is 15.00.

You can also select the row by clicking the row designator, then using the Row option on the **Format** menu to achieve the same result.

Task 8: Entering numeric data

This is the same procedure as for cell labels.

1   Activate cell C3 and type the number 0.

2   Press *Enter*. The number is aligned to the right of the cell.

Make sure that this is the number 0 and not the letter O (a common source of error).

3   Complete the other income and expenditure items as shown in FIGURE 2.9; use the *Enter* key or down arrow key to complete each entry. *Don't attempt to calculate the totals yet.*

To amend the data use the same procedures as in Tasks 2–5 above.

Optional: If you are *not* proceeding to the next activity then save and close the workbook. Saving is covered in detail later in this unit, in Task 16. For the moment proceed as follows in Task 9. It is assumed throughout these units that you wish to save your work to a diskette (A drive). If not then substitute the appropriate drive letter for A drive.

Task 9: Saving the workbook

1   Open the **File** menu (click **File** on the Menu Bar) and select the **Save as** option.

A dialog box appears – see FIGURE 2.8.

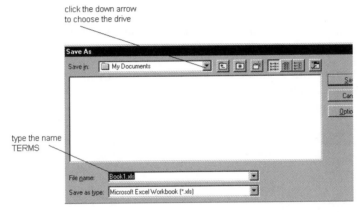

FIGURE 2.8

At the moment the workbook has the default name **BOOK1.XLS** – see the **File Name** box at the bottom of the dialog box. (The .XLS extension may not appear.)

2   First make sure that you have a suitable, formatted floppy disk in the diskette drive.

Click the down arrow button on the **Save in:** box and select **3½ Floppy [A:]** from the list offered.

3   Click the **File name** box to select it and amend the file name to **TERMS** (double click the file name to select it if necessary and type over the top, upper or lower case).

If you have made a mistake click the Cancel button and start again, otherwise click the Save button.

The file takes a few seconds to save to A drive – a 'saving' message is displayed at the bottom of the worksheet and the drive light should come on to confirm this .

4   When you return to your workbook you will see the name of the workbook, **TERMS.XLS,** displayed in the title bar.

5   To quit Excel open the **File** menu and select **Exit**.

You will be returned to the Windows 95 desktop.

6   If you wish to exit Windows 95 then click the █Start█ button on the Taskbar and select Shut Down.

Task 10: Using formulae

Formulae are used to perform a variety of operations including calculations. A formula is placed in a cell in the same way as text or numbers. It can be very simple, such as adding the contents of two cells, or complex, containing mathematical or financial functions.

You must always start a formula with an equals (=) sign; it tells Excel that you are about to apply a formula to a cell.

 If you are not continuing from the previous task then you will need to open the workbook **TERMS** created earlier. Make sure that Sheet1 is the active sheet. Refer to Task 17 'Loading an existing workbook' for guidance if necessary.

	A	B	C	D	E	F
1			PERSONAL FINANCES - TERM 1			
2	INCOME		Week 1			
3	Opening Bals		0			
4	Grant		500			
5	Bank Loan		400			
6	Parents		300			
7	Total Income					
8						
9	EXPENDITURE					
10	Accommodation		60			
11	Food and Travel		30			
12	Books		75			
13	Other		20			
14	Total Expenditure					
15						

FIGURE 2.9

1   **Addition**   Now that we have entered the first week's income and expenditure figures we can add them using formulae – refer to FIGURE 2.9 if necessary.

To calculate total income, first activate cell C7 and type an = sign. The = sign appears in the formula bar, alongside four buttons, including a 'tick' ✓ and a 'cross' ✕ button.

2   Type the formula **SUM(C3:C6)** next to the = sign (see FIGURE 2.10). This is the formula to add or sum the range of four cells C3 to C6. Functions and formulae may be typed in upper or lower case.

3   Click the **tick** ✓ button next to the formula (or press *Enter*). The results of the formula are displayed in cell C7 – the income total of 1200.

If you make a mistake entering the formula or get an error message, you can edit or delete it. Make sure that the appropriate cell (e.g. C7) is selected, then:

Delete – use the *Delete* key to delete the entire cell contents;

Edit – move the mouse pointer to the appropriate character in the cell and double click. Use the *Backspace* or *Delete* key to delete. Click the tick button again, or press the *Enter* key.

formula also appears
in the Formula Bar

	▾	✗ ✓ =	=SUM(C3:C6)			
	A	B	C	D	E	F
1			PERSONAL FINANCES - TERM 1			
2	INCOME		Week1			
3	Opening Bals		0			
4	Grant		500			
5	Bank Loan		400			
6	Parents		300			
7	Total Income		=SUM(C3:C6)			
8						

formula entered in
the cell

FIGURE 2.10

Notes on the Sum Function. SUM is an Excel *function* and is a lot quicker than typing the full formula =C3+C4+C5+C6. SUM is also expandable. If another row is inserted into this range of 4 cells at a later stage, say between rows 4 and 5, the new cell would automatically be included in the range. This is not the case if you type the formula out in full using the + sign.

Task 11: Adding up columns – shortcuts

We will now use a formula to add up the total expenditure.

1   Activate cell C14 and type =SUM(

2   Move the screen pointer to the first expenditure item, cell C10.

3   Hold down the mouse button and drag the pointer down to cell C13. Four cells are enclosed by a dotted box – see FIGURE 2.11.

The formula bar should read **SUM(C10:C13**

If you have made a mistake then click the cross (✗) box on the formula bar and start again.

4   Click the tick box and the result of the formula – 185 – is displayed. There is no need to type the final bracket.

9	EXPENDITURE	
10	Accommodation	60
11	Food and Travel	30
12	Books	75
13	Other	20
14	Total Expenditure	=sum(C10:C13

— cells enclosed in box

FIGURE 2.11

Task 12: Amending formulae – error messages

Try the following.

1 Activate cell C7 and move the pointer onto the Formula Bar; it reads **SUM(C3:C6)**

2 Alter the formula to **SUM(C3:C7)** and click the tick box to execute the new formula.

An error dialog box appears. As **C7** is the 'destination' cell – the cell containing the formula – it cannot also be one of the cells to be summed as this is 'circular'.

3 Click the Cancel button on the dialog box.

4 Correct the formula to its original **SUM(C3:C6)** and execute it again.

Note: When you edit a formula Excel's 'Range Finder' feature highlights the cell range in colour, both for the formula and for the cells in the worksheet.

5 Excel has a range of error messages, we'll look at one more for the moment.

Activate cell C14 and amend **SUM** to **SIM** in the Formula Bar.

6 Execute this formula (use the *Enter* key or tick box)

The error message #NAME? appears in the cell. Make sure that the cell is still selected but don't correct it just yet.

Task 13: Clearing cell contents

1 Move the screen pointer to the Menu Bar at the top of the screen.

2 Click the **Edit** menu to select it.

The Edit menu opens.

3 Select the **Clear** then the **All** option.

The cell is cleared.

 NB you can use the *Delete* key instead of the **Clear** command.

Task 14: Adding columns – the AutoSum button

The `AutoSum` button offers the quickest way of adding a column of figures. It is on the Standard tool bar and is marked with the Greek letter Sigma (like a capital M on its side – see key at end of unit).

1 We need to add the expenditure cells again; use the dragging technique used in Task 11 above to select the cell range C10 to C14 (see note below).

2 Click the `AutoSum` button once and the SUM formula is executed. The total of 185 appears in cell C14.

A note on AutoCalculate.

Whenever you select a range of cells holding numeric data Excel will automatically tell you the sum of their values in the bottom right hand corner of the window. This is for information only and is not executed until you enter a SUM formula.

Task 15: Subtraction formulae

We now need to subtract total expenditure from total income to find the closing balance for week 1.

1 Enter this cell label in cell A16 – see FIGURE 2.12.

2 Activate cell C16 and type the formula *=C7-C14*

3 Execute the formula as before. The closing balance for week 1 (1015) appears in cell C16. Your worksheet should now be the same as FIGURE 2.12.

	A	B	C	D
3	Opening Bals		0	
4	Grant		500	
5	Bank Loan		400	
6	Parents		300	
7	Total Income		1200	
8				
9	EXPENDITURE			
10	Accommodation		60	
11	Food and Travel		30	
12	Books		75	
13	Other		20	
14	Total Expenditure		185	
15				
16	CLOSING BALS.		1015	
17				

FIGURE 2.12

Task 16: Saving your workbook

If you have continued straight on from the previous task then at the moment your workbook is only saved in the computer's main memory. It could be lost for ever if your PC crashes or the power goes off. You need to save it permanently as a named file on disk. In these units, I make the assumption that you will want to save your work on a diskette (A drive) not on the computer's hard disk (e.g. C drive). All future references assume this.

 If you have already saved the workbook as **TERMS** then open the **File** menu and select **Save** (*not* **Save as**) to save the present version and continue with the next activity. You can also use the Save button on the Standard Toolbar to save.

1   Open the **File** menu (click **File** on the Menu Bar) and select the **Save As** option. A dialog box appears – see FIGURE 2.13.

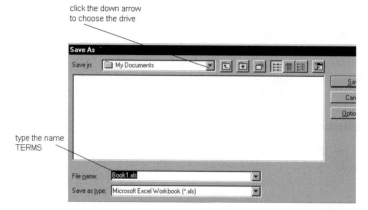

FIGURE 2.13

At the moment the workbook has the default name **BOOK1.XLS** – see the **File Name** box. **.XLS** is an *extension* automatically assigned to all Excel workbook files, but we want to save it under a more meaningful name than **BOOK1**. (**Note:** The **.XLS** extension may not appear on your screen.)

A filename can be up to 218 characters long, and can consist of any combination of letters, numbers and certain special characters including spaces, dashes and underscores but not the following: \ / < > * ? " ; or :

2   First make sure that you have a suitable, formatted floppy disk in the diskette drive.

3   Click the down arrow button on the **Save in:** box and select 3$\frac{1}{2}$ **Floppy** [A:] from the list offered.

4   Amend the file name to **TERMS** (double click the file name box to select it if necessary and type over the top).

5   If you have made a mistake click the Cancel button and start again, otherwise click the Save button.

6   The **Summary Information** dialog box may appear next, allowing you to save further information about the workbook; the author's name is already completed. We won't use this feature yet; click the Cancel button.

The file takes a few seconds to save to A drive – the Status Bar shows the save process and the drive light should come on to confirm this.

7   When you return to your workbook you will see the name of the workbook, **TERMS.XLS**, displayed in the title bar.

Get into the habit of saving your document regularly as you work, not just when you exit Excel. Use the **Save** not the **Save as** command to save an existing File (**Save as** is used to save a new workbook, or an existing workbook under a new name).

Remember that any data keyed in since your last Save command has not yet been saved permanently.

8   At this point use the **File** menu and select **Exit** to exit from Excel.

Task 17: Loading an existing workbook

Your workbook **TERMS** has been saved to disk as an Excel file on A drive. To work on it again you must use this name to retrieve it from disk and load it into the main memory.

1   Start Excel again. A new blank workbook appears with the default name **BOOK1**. We will close it as we want to work on an existing workbook. Open the **File** menu and select the **Close** option (*not* **Exit**). The document window goes blank, as no workbook is in use.

2   If you saved your **TERMS** workbook to a diskette then obviously the first step is to ensure that this disk is in drive A. Open the **File** menu and select **Open**. A dialog box appears – see FIGURE 2.14.

It is similar to the **Save as** dialog box shown in FIGURE 2.13.

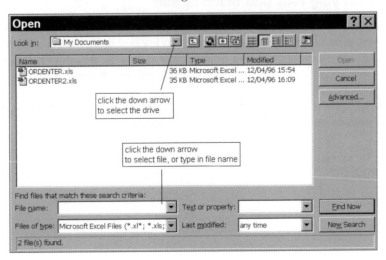

FIGURE 2.14

3 If you are sure of the file name and the drive, then simply type them in the **File Name** box – it is already selected.

4 Type **A:\TERMS** and click the `Open` button. The file will load from disk and appear on screen. If not, check your spelling (especially the colon and the back slash) and that you are using the correct diskette.

5 Open the **File** menu and select the Close option again.

Task 18: Retrieving a file from the file list

Alternatively you can open a file by choosing it from a list.

1 Open the **File** menu and select the **Open** option. The **Open** dialog box opens again. This time we may need to select the drive – see FIGURE 2.14 above.

2 Move the screen pointer onto the **Look in:** box and click the `Down Arrow` button. Select the 3$\frac{1}{2}$ **Floppy** [A:] drive icon. The workbook **TERMS.XLS** is listed in the dialog box.

3 Click it to select it if necessary, then click the `Open` button again. The file will load from disk and appear on screen.

Independent Activity. Close the workbook as before. Open the **File** menu again and look at the bottom of the menu. You should see the workbook listed near the bottom of the menu. Click it to load the workbook again. Excel remembers the last four workbooks that you (or another user of the application) have used.

Task 19: Copying cells and deleting data

At the moment we only have data for one week . We are going to copy this data into the next column to create week 2, and modify certain cells. We will then experiment with a number of ways to move, copy, and delete cells. They are all useful in certain contexts, so make sure that you try out all these activities.

1 This involves selecting one or more cells, and then copying them to another part of the worksheet. Select all the cells containing the week 1 data.

2 Move the screen pointer onto cell C2, and drag down to column C16 – see FIGURE 2.15.

	A	B	C	D
1			PERSONAL FINANCE	
2	INCOME		Week1	
3	Opening Bals		0	
4	Grant		500	
5	Bank Loan		400	
6	Parents		300	
7	Total Income		1200	
8				
9	EXPENDITURE			
10	Accommodation		60	
11	Food and Travel		30	
12	Books		75	
13	Other		20	
14	Total Expenditure		185	
15				
16	CLOSING BALS		1015	

FIGURE 2.15

If you select the wrong cells then merely click anywhere on the worksheet to remove the selection and try again

3   Open the **Edit** menu and select **Copy** (*not* **Cut**).

The selected area is now enclosed by a flowing dotted line called the Marquee.

4   **Pasting.** Next we must indicate where the cells are to be copied to.

Activate cell D2 – the cell where you want to start pasting from.

5   Open the **Edit** menu and select **Paste**.

The cells are copied to a new location, and the Marquee remains around the area that you copied, allowing you to paste it again if you wish.

6   Remove the Marquee by pressing the *Esc* key on the keyboard.

Notes

Whenever you copy cells, Excel stores them in a temporary memory area called the Clipboard. They stay there until they are replaced by some other Copy or Cut command.

If you have made a mistake then open the **Edit** menu and select the Undo Paste command. (or click the Undo button) You can undo up to your last 16 actions.

Notice that not only the data but also the formulae are copied. Excel automatically adjusts the cell references in the formulae to refer to their new location in Column D. For this reason they are called *relative references*. Click the cells D7, D14 and D16 and check their formulae in the Formula Bar.

7   **Cutting and pasting**. Cutting cells physically removes them from their original location so that they can be pasted to a new one. It is similar operation to copying.

Select the cells for week 2 now, i.e. cell range **D2** to **D16**.

8   Open the **Edit** menu and select the **Cut** option; (*not* **Copy**). The cells are surrounded by the marquee as before.

9   Activate cell E2, then open the **Edit** menu and select **Paste**. This time the column is moved a column to the right, leaving column D blank.

 You may use the Cut, Copy and Paste tools on the Tool Bar instead of menu commands – see the Toolbar key at the end of this unit.

10   Clearing ranges of cells: Let's now clear the copied column. In the next section we will learn a better way of copying columns using the **Fill** command.

Select the cells in column E again if necessary.

 11   Open the **Edit** menu and select **Clear.** Then **All.**

As before, you can use the **Edit-Undo** command to restore deleted data. You can undo up to your last 16 actions.

12   **Copying cells using Edit-Fill-Righ**t. Move the screen pointer onto cell C2.

13   Hold down the mouse button and drag down the column to cell C16.

14   *Keeping the mouse button pressed down,* drag the screen pointer across to select the same number of cells in the next column. Now let go.

You should now have selected two columns – see FIGURE 2.16.

	A	B	C	D
1			PERSONAL FINANCE	
2	INCOME		Week 1	
3	Opening Bals		0	
4	Grant		500	
5	Bank Loan		400	
6	Parents		300	
7	Total Income		1200	
8				
9	EXPENDITURE			
10	Accommodation		60	
11	Food and Travel		30	
12	Books		75	
13	Other		20	
14	Total Expenditure		185	
15				
16	CLOSING BALS.		1015	

FIGURE 2.16

You may need to try more than once to get it right.

15   Now open the **Edit** menu and select **Fill** then **Right**. The contents of column C – data and formulae – are copied to column D. If the copying is incorrect then open the **Edit** menu again and select **Undo-Fill-Right**.

16 Select cell D2 and amend the column label to **'Week 2'**. The values in cells D4 to D6 for **Grant, Loan** and **Parents** will need to be deleted; they are 'one-off' income items only applying to week 1.

17 Drag from D4 down to D6 to select these three cells.

18 Press the _Delete_ key.

Notice how the totals in column D are automatically re-calculated. (If you have cleared the wrong cells then open the **Edit** menu again and select **Undo Clear**.)

Notice that your closing balance for week 2 is now a negative amount, an insolvent –185 in cell D16. However this is because we have not yet carried forward the closing balance of 1015 from week 1 to the opening balance for week 2.

Let's do this with a formula.

19 We want the value in cell D3, the opening balance for week 2, to equal C16, the closing balance for week 1.

20 Activate cell D3 and type **=C16**.

21 Click the [Tick] button to execute the formula. The week 2 totals are recalculated – your closing balance for week 2 is now a healthy 830.

22 Now make the following amendments to week 2

Food and Travel 35

Books 15.

The closing balance is now 885.

23 We can now use week 2 as our model for the next three weeks.

Select the week *2* values and the *three adjacent* columns, i.e. four columns in all, cells D3 – G16 (see FIGURE 2.17).

Week 2			
1015			
1015			
60			
35			
15			
20			
130			
885			

FIGURE 2.17

24 Use the **Edit-Fill-Right** command as before. The contents of column D (week 2) are copied into columns E, F and G. The closing balance at the end of week 5 should be 495 in cell G16 – see FIGURE 2.18.

	A	B	C	D	E	F	G
1			PERSONAL FINANCES - TERM 1				
2	INCOME		Week 1	Week 2			
3	Opening Bals		0	1015	885	755	625
4	Grant		500				
5	Bank Loan		400				
6	Parents		300				
7	Total Income		1200	1015	885	755	625
8							
9	EXPENDITURE						
10	Accommodation		60	60	60	60	60
11	Food and Travel		30	35	35	35	35
12	Books		75	15	15	15	15
13	Other		20	20	20	20	20
14	Total Expenditure		185	130	130	130	130
15							
16	CLOSING BALS.		1015	885	755	625	495

FIGURE 2.18

Use the **Undo** command, as before if you make a mistake.

25 Remember to save the changes that you have made – use **Save** (*not Save as*) on the **File** menu.

Task 20: Using AutoFill to complete a series

Rather than typing in week numbers 3 – 5 in cells in cells D3 to F3 we can use AutoFill to complete the series.

1 Click cell D2 to select it.

Notice that in the bottom right-hand corner of the cell there is a small 'handle'.

2 Move the mouse pointer onto the handle. Notice that it becomes cross-shaped – see FIGURE 2.19.

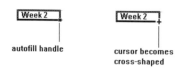

autofill handle   cursor becomes
                       cross-shaped

FIGURE 2.19

3 Now drag the cursor to enclose cells D2 to G2 as well.

4 Let go of the mouse button. These cells are correctly labelled.

If you are not continuing with the next unit then save and close the workbook.

Summary of commands

Menu commands show the menu name first, followed by the command to choose from the menu, e.g. Edit-Clear means open the **Edit** menu and select the **Clear** command.

Edit-Clear	Clear cell contents
Edit-Copy	Copy selected cells
Edit-Cut	Remove selected cells
Edit-Delete	Delete selected rows or columns
Edit-Delete Sheet	Delete selected worksheet
Edit-Fill-Right	Copy selected cells into selected right hand columns
Edit-Paste	Insert cut or copied cells at a specified location
Edit-Undo	Undo previous operation(s)
File-Close	Close current workbook
File-Exit	Exit Excel
File-New	Open new, blank workbook
File-Open	Retrieve an existing workbook
File-Save as	Save and name a new workbook
File-Save	Save an existing workbook
Format	Format column, rows etc
Help	Select Help
Tools-Autocorrect	Correct misspelled words automatically

Functions

=SUM()	Add a range of cells

Standard Toolbar

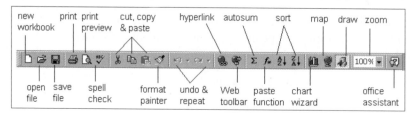

Formatting Toolbar

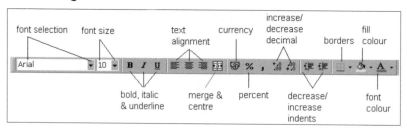

Summary of unit

In this unit you have learned how to:

■ enter data into a worksheet

■ correct the data using the Toolbar and the menu bar

■ edit cell contents with and without using the formula bar

■ widen columns by dragging the mouse and by using the **Format** menu

■ alter the height of rows by dragging the mouse

■ save and close the workbook

■ use formulae for calculations, particularly the SUM function and the AutoSum button

■ amend formulae using the formula bar

■ remove the data from cells using the **Edit** menu

■ load an existing workbook by typing the name and by using the file list

■ copy and cut cells and paste them

■ use the **Edit-Fill-Right** command to copy cells.

Formatting, printing and copying your worksheet

What you will learn in this unit

By the end of this unit you will be able to

- format a worksheet
- print a worksheet
- copy a worksheet
- test assumptions by altering values.

What you should know already

Before you start this unit, make sure you can do the following.

Skill	Covered in
Open a workbook and use simple commands	Unit 1
Enter and delete worksheet data	Unit 2
Open, close and save a workbook	Unit 2

What you need

To complete this unit, you will need

- the workbook **TERMS** created in Units 1 and 2.

Introduction

You now have a valid working model of the first five weeks' finances for a college term. In this unit you will learn how to format your worksheet. Excel allows you to alter the worksheet format in many ways, including the type size and style, and text alignment. You will also learn how to use printer and page settings.

If you are not continuing from the previous unit then you will need to open the workbook **TERMS**. (Use the File menu and select Open – see Unit 2, 'Loading an existing workbook', Task 17). Make sure that Sheet1 is the active sheet.

Task 1: Emboldening

First we will put the title and cell labels in bold.

3 Formatting, printing and copying your worksheet

1 Drag to select the title and the column headings – cells A1 to G2. (see FIGURE 3.1)

	A	B	C	D	E	F	G
1			PERSONAL FINANCES - TERM 1				
2	INCOME		Week 1	Week 2	Week 3	Week 4	Week 5
3	Opening Bals		0	1015	885	755	625
4	Grant		500				
5	Bank Loan		400				
6	Parents		300				
7	Total Income		1200	1015	885	755	625
8							
9	EXPENDITURE						
10	Accommodation		60	60	60	60	60
11	Food and Travel		30	35	35	35	35
12	Books		75	15	15	15	15
13	Other		20	20	20	20	20
14	Total Expenditure		185	130	130	130	130
15							
16	CLOSING BALS.		1015	885	755	625	495

FIGURE 3.1

2 Click the **Bold** button on the Formatting Tool Bar – marked with a capital **B** (see FIGURE 3.2). The cells are emboldened. (You may also wish to use the *Italic* or Underline buttons, marked with capital *I* or U.)

3 Now select the row labels in column 1 and embolden them in the same way.

You may need to widen column A now, in which case open the **Format** menu and select the **Column** then the **AutoFit** options. Repeat this operation to embolden the closing balances in row 16.

Task 2: Character size and fonts

1 Select all the row labels in column A again.

2 Click the **Font Size** button – see FIGURE 3.2.

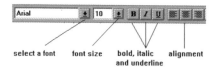

select a font   font size   bold, italic   alignment
                             and underline

FIGURE 3.2

At the moment all characters on the worksheet are the default size of 10 point.

3 Click 8 – you may need to scroll it into view.

The cell labels are now in a smaller font.

 You may also like to experiment with different fonts or typefaces, using the **Font** button – see FIGURE 3.2. Ones that are not available are shown in pale grey rather than black.

Task 3: Alignment

At the moment the numeric values are aligned to the right of the cells. This is the default for numbers. It can look neater to centre them under the column headings.

1   Select all the cells containing numeric data , i.e. cells C3 to G16.

2   On the Formatting Tool Bar are a group of 3 alignment buttons, showing left, centre and right alignment – see FIGURE 3.2 above.

Click the **Centre** button. The values are centred.

Task 4: Number and currency formats

Let's alter the way numeric values are displayed. Select all the numeric cells again if necessary (C3 – G16).

1   Open the **Format** menu and select the **Cells** option.

The **Format Cells** dialog box is displayed.

2   Select the **Number** tab if necessary – see FIGURE 3.3.

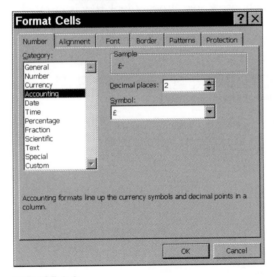

FIGURE 3.3

3   Select the **Accounting** option from the **Category** list.

The format shown in FIGURE 3.3 above displays numbers to two decimal places, and the £ currency symbol.

4   Click the **OK** button and the cells are reformatted.

Troubleshooting You may need to widen some columns if a row of hash (#) symbols are shown – see Unit 2, Task 6.

3 Formatting, printing and copying your worksheet

 Always use the **Format Cells** option to add currency symbols and other types of number formatting. *Do not* enter currency symbols directly. If you do this then Excel will regard the values as text, not numbers, and be unable to use them in calculations.

Task 5: Inserting and deleting columns and rows

1 Click the column designator at the top of column B (i.e. the capital B). This selects the whole column.

2 Open the **Edit** menu and select **Delete**. Column B is deleted and subsequent columns are shifted to the left. All the cell references and formulae are automatically adjusted to reflect their new position.

 Removing a blank column should cause no problems, but removing a column containing data and formulae obviously could. You can select **Undo** from the **Edit** column if you delete the wrong column or row.

3 Now let's insert an extra row; click the row designator for Row 2. The whole row is selected.

4 Open the **Insert** menu and choose **Rows**. A new blank row is inserted.

The worksheet has a neater and more balanced appearance and should now look like FIGURE 3.4.

	A	B	C	D	E	F
1		PERSONAL FINANCES - TERM 1				
2						
3	INCOME	week 1	week 2	week 3	week 4	week 5
4	Opening Bals	£ -	£ 1,015.00	£ 885.00	£ 755.00	£ 625.00
5	Grant	£ 500.00				
6	Bank Loan	£ 400.00				
7	Parents	£ 300.00				
8	Total Income	£ 1,200.00	£ 1,015.00	£ 885.00	£ 755.00	£ 625.00
9						
10	EXPENDITURE					
11	Accommodation	£ 60.00	£ 60.00	£ 60.00	£ 60.00	£ 60.00
12	Food and Travel	£ 30.00	£ 35.00	£ 35.00	£ 35.00	£ 35.00
13	Books	£ 75.00	£ 15.00	£ 15.00	£ 15.00	£ 15.00
14	Other	£ 20.00	£ 20.00	£ 20.00	£ 20.00	£ 20.00
15	Total Expenditure	£ 185.00	£ 130.00	£ 130.00	£ 130.00	£ 130.00
16						
17	Closing Bals	£ 1,015.00	£ 885.00	£ 755.00	£ 625.00	£ 495.00

FIGURE 3.4

Task 6: Centring the title

It would look neater to centre the title across columns A to F – the area of the worksheet that will eventually be printed.

1 Select cell range 1A to 1F

2 Click the `Merge and Centre` button on the Formatting Toolbar, it is marked with a small 'a' – see key at the end of this unit. The title is centred across the columns selected – however cell range 1A to 1F are now treated as one merged cell and cannot be selected individually. If this causes a problem then you will need to remove the centring – see Notes below.

Notes

If you decide to widen the worksheet later you will need to re-centre the title. To restore the default alignment, select the cells, open the **Format** menu and select the **Cells** option, and then click the `Alignment` tab.

Click the **Merge Cells** box to deselect it.

Task 7: Adding borders

Borders can be used to mark off various sections of the worksheet and make it easier to read – see FIGURE 3.6 below. First let's draw a single line to mark off different sections of the worksheet.

1 Select cells A9 to F9.

2 Open the **Format** menu and select **Cells.** The Format Cells dialog box opens.

3 Click the `Border` tab. New options are shown – see FIGURE 3.5 below for the options to select:

4 Select the **Outline** option from the **Presets** section.

5 Select the **Thin Line** option from the **Style** box.

6 Click the `OK` button.

   This places a single line at the bottom of row 9.

7 Click to remove the highlight from the cells.

8 Next we will put a thicker line around all the worksheet data. Select cell A1 and drag the screen pointer down to cell F17.

9 Open the **Format** menu again and select **Cells.**

   The **Format Cells** dialog box appears, click the `Border` tab if necessary.

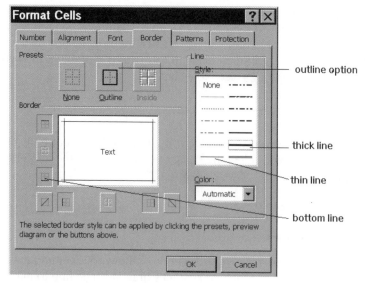

FIGURE 3.5

10 Select the Thick Line option in the Style box – see FIGURE 3.5.

11 Select the Outline option from the Presets section.

12 Click the OK button. You are returned to the worksheet.

13 Click to remove the highlight from the cells. The worksheet is enclosed in a thick line.

 Troubleshooting – removing unwanted borders Use the same commands, i.e. select the relevant cells, and select Cells from the Format menu. Then click the relevant style button to deselect the unwanted border.

Independent activity

The Formatting Toolbar supplies a Borders button. Identify it and click the down arrow button; use it to

■ draw a single line under cells A16 to F16

■ give the cells in column A a single right hand border.

 Remember that you can use the Edit-Undo command to undo any formatting.

Task 8: Gridline display

The gridlines marking the cell boundaries can be turned off to emphasise the borders that we have drawn.

1 Open the Tools menu and choose Options. A dialog box opens. Make sure that the View tab is selected.

2   Click the ▌Gridlines▐ button. The tick disappears as this option is deselected.

3   Click the ▌OK▐ button. The gridlines disappear. This will not prevent the gridlines displaying when the worksheet is printed. Your worksheet should now look like FIGURE 3.6.

	A	B	C	D	E	F
1			PERSONAL FINANCES - TERM 1			
2						
3	INCOME	Week 1	Week 2	Week 3	Week 4	Week 5
4	Opening Bals	£ -	£ 1,015.00	£ 885.00	£ 755.00	£ 625.00
5	Grant	£ 500.00				
6	Bank Loan	£ 400.00				
7	Parents	£ 300.00				
8	Total Income	£1,200.00	£ 1,015.00	£ 885.00	£ 755.00	£ 625.00
9						
10	EXPENDITURE					
11	Accommodation	£ 60.00	£ 60.00	£ 60.00	£ 60.00	£ 60.00
12	Food and Travel	£ 30.00	£ 35.00	£ 35.00	£ 35.00	£ 35.00
13	Books	£ 75.00	£ 15.00	£ 15.00	£ 15.00	£ 15.00
14	Other	£ 20.00	£ 20.00	£ 20.00	£ 20.00	£ 20.00
15	Total Expenditure	£ 185.00	£ 130.00	£ 130.00	£ 130.00	£ 130.00
16						
17	CLOSING BALS.	£1,015.00	£ 885.00	£ 755.00	£ 625.00	£ 495.00

FIGURE 3.6

Task 9: Freezing titles and labels

We will add a note to the bottom of the worksheet. This means that the worksheet will become too large to view all at once. Before one scrolls to another part of the worksheet it is possible to 'freeze' both the titles and the column and row labels so that they are always in view, and so keep a track of what each row or column represents.

1   Click cell B4.

2   Open the Window menu and select the Freeze Panes option. All cells above and to the left of this cell are frozen.

Try scrolling across and down; the column and row labels stay there as a constant reference.

3   To unfreeze panes, open the Window menu and select Unfreeze Panes.

Task 10: Entering and justifying blocks of text

Although Excel does not offer full word processing facilities, blocks of text, such as brief notes, can be added to worksheets.

1   Click the ▌Text Box▐ button on the Drawing Toolbar which is at the bottom of the Window (see key at the end of this unit). If it is not displayed then open the View menu and select the Toolbars option.

2   Now move the screen pointer to cell C19.

3   Drag to draw a text box large enough to hold the text shown in FIGURE 3.7.

PERSONAL FINANCES - TERM 1

Week 1	Week 2	Week 3	Week 4	Week 5
£ 30.00	£ 35.00	£ 35.00	£ 35.00	£ 35.00
£ 75.00	£ 15.00	£ 15.00	£ 15.00	£ 15.00
£ 20.00	£ 20.00	£ 20.00	£ 20.00	£ 20.00
£ 185.00	£ 130.00	£130.00	£130.00	£130.00
£1,015.00	£ 885.00	£755.00	£625.00	£495.00

Worksheet showing the income and expenditure for the first 5 weeks of the Autumn Term

selection handle - drag to re-size box

box can be deleted when border is dotted

FIGURE 3.7

Type in the text – it is aligned into the text box.

Notes

If the text box is selected, it may be

- moved by dragging the border

- re-sized by dragging one of the small selection handles

- deleted provided that the border is dotted, rather than diagonal lines (see FIGURE 3.7) by pressing the *Delete* key.

Text within the box can be edited, emboldened, etc in the usual ways.

Task 11: Adding arrows and shapes to a worksheet

You can also emphasise a key point in your worksheet by circling it or using an arrow to point to it. Let's try this, using FIGURE 3.8 as a guide.

	A	B	C	D	E	F
1		PERSONAL FINANCES - TERM 1				
2						
3	INCOME	Week 1	Week 2	Week 3	Week 4	Week 5
13	Books	£ 75.00	£ 15.00	£ 15.00	£ 15.00	£ 15.00
14	Other	£ 20.00	£ 20.00	£ 20.00	£ 20.00	£ 20.00
15	Total Expenditure	£ 185.00	£ 130.00	£130.00	£130.00	£130.00
16						
17	CLOSING BALS.	£1,015.00	£ 885.00	£755.00	£625.00	£495.00
18						
19		Worksheet showing the				
20		income and expenditure for the				
21		first 5 weeks of the Autumn		On Target!		
22		Term				

FIGURE 3.8

1   Click the ▮Oval▮ button on the Drawing Toolbar. If the toolbar is not displayed then open the **View** menu and select the Toolbars option.

2   Use the mouse pointer to encircle cell F17. If the cell becomes invisible don't worry – see below.

3   Click the `Arrow` button and draw the arrow.

4   Finally use the `Text Box` button to draw a text box large enough to hold the text shown in FIGURE 3.7. Remember that you can delete a selected object by pressing the *Delete* key.

5   Now scroll the worksheet. You should find that the objects that you have drawn are attached to their underlying cells and move with them.

If the cell is invisible

■ click the oval object to select it

■ open the **Format** menu and choose the **AutoShape** option

■ choose the `Colours and Lines` tab

■ in the dialog box that appears, click the `down arrow` button on the **Fill-Color** box

■ select `No Fill` then `OK`.

Task 12: Viewing the full screen

1   Open the **View** menu and select **Full Screen**. This enlarges the worksheet to its fullest extent, allowing you to see the maximum number of rows. However other useful components such as the toolbars and the Taskbar are hidden.

2   Issue the command again to reinstate them

Task 13: Setting the print area

To print a worksheet you must give Excel instructions on what and how to print – which cells, number of copies, and so on.

1   **Selecting the print area**. First select the entire worksheet area that you want to print – cells A1 to G22 – you may find it easier to select a large range of cells as follows. Click cell A1 – the top left of the area that you want to select.

2   Scroll down the worksheet until you can see cell G22.

3   Hold down the **_Shift_** key. There is one on either side of the keyboard, marked with an upwards arrow.

4   Select cell G22 – the bottom right of the range that you want to select. The whole cell range is selected.

5   **Setting the print area**. Open the **File** menu and select the **Print Area** option.

6   Select the **Set print Area** option. The print area is surrounded with a dotted line.

If no print area has been set then the default area is the printed page, e.g. A4.

7 **Printing.** Open the **File** menu and select **Print**. The **Print** dialog box appears.

8 Click the Active Sheets button in the **Print What** section. The print area of the selected worksheet will be printed, not any blank areas outside it. This is important when the worksheet becomes larger.

9 Before you print, click the Preview button which shows how the worksheet will look when printed on an A4 page.

Task 14: Page Settings

1 Click the Setup button at the top of the Preview window. The **Page Setup** dialog box appears – make sure that the **Sheet** option is displayed – see FIGURE 3.9.

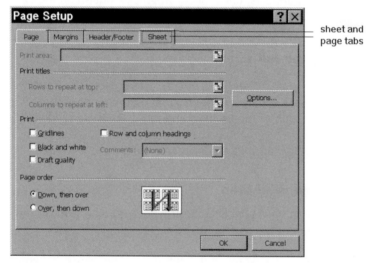

FIGURE 3.9

2 Make sure that two boxes '**Row and Column Headings**' and '**Gridlines**' are both unchecked, i.e. there is no tick in either of them. It is usual to print a worksheet without the row and column headings and gridlines, if it is not too large or detailed.

3 Next click the Page tab on the **Page Setup** dialog box – see FIGURE 3.9 above – a new set of options are displayed. Your printer may offer the following settings, if so they will appear in black rather than pale grey. Check the following.

■ Orientation: normally worksheets are printed in *portrait*, i.e. vertically down the page. Wide worksheets can be printed in *landscape* – horizontally across the page.

■ Paper size: the current paper size is displayed, normally A4.

- Scaling: You can adjust the size of the printed area to fit the paper size.

- Fit to: will adjust the size of the printed area to fit on one or more pages.

4 Margins and alignment. Now click the Margins tab. A new set of options are displayed.

5 Click the **Horizontally** and **Vertically** boxes. They will centre the printout on the page.

Task 15: Headers and footers

1 Now click the Header/Footer tab.

   Headers and footers can be added to the top and bottom of every printed page. The default ones are the sheet and page numbers but you can create your own. Let's add the date and your name.

2 Click the Custom Header button and a further dialog box appears – see FIGURE 3.10.

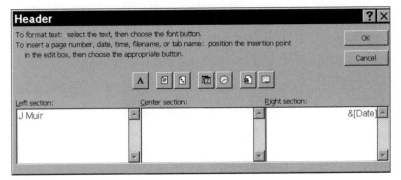

FIGURE 3.10

It is divided into three sections – left, right and centre aligned.

3 Select the left section and type in your name.

4 Select the right section and click the date button – use the Help button (marked with a ?) if you need to identify it. The dialog box should now look like FIGURE 3.10.

5 Click OK .

6 Now click the Custom Footer button. Insert the page number if necessary.

7 Click OK .You are returned to the main **Page Setup** dialog box. Click OK again.

Task 16: Printing a worksheet

1   Make sure that the printer is

 - switched on

 - set online – check switch and warning light

 - connected via cable to your computer

 - supplied with paper.

Check these in turn if the next section does not produce a printout.

2   Open **Print Preview** again if necessary.

The Print Preview screen appears. You can now see the headers and footers. There are various options along the top of the screen. Do not use any of these options for now, they are for information only.

 - **Next** and **Previous** are for multi-page worksheets.

 - **Margins** displays the current margin settings.

 - **Page Break Preview** allows you to reset both the print area and the page breaks simply by dragging them. You can also cut and paste between different printed pages. Excel will then automatically re-scale the cells to fit.

 - **Print** and **Setup** allow you to either proceed with printing or go back to the **Page Setup** menus.

3   Now move the screen pointer over the printed area.

It changes to a magnifying glass shape.

4   Click and the area under the pointer is enlarged.

You can scroll around to look at other parts of the worksheet.

The Zoom button will return you to full page mode.

5   Now finally if you are happy with the print preview, click the Print button at the top of the screen.

If you are not happy then the Close button will cancel printing.

6   Click OK on the **Print** dialog box if necessary.

The worksheet should start printing now.

 Troubleshooting If your worksheet won't print check the previous stages again.

7   Finally check that the correct printer is selected as follows.

■ Open the **File** menu and select the **Print** option again.

■ Check in the Printer section that the correct printer is selected.

If the print area is incorrect then you will need to remove it and reset it:

■ select the menu options File-Print Area-Clear Print Area

■ the dotted print area line reverts to the page default – see Task 13 above.

8 Save and close the workbook.

Task 17: Consolidation – check your progress

We are going to extend the worksheet to cover a 10-week term. The instructions will be kept to a minimum, as you have already practised the operations involved.

1 Retrieve the **TERMS** workbook if necessary. Make sure that Sheet1 is selected

2 First select the week 5 column, i.e. cells F3-F17 and keep the mouse button pressed down.

3 Drag across the worksheet to select the next 5 columns G to K. These will hold the data for weeks 6-10.

4 Now use the **Edit-Fill-Right** command to copy the data across.

Remember that you can always use the **Undo** command if you make a mistake.

5 Some minor amendments need to be made next.

■ amend the week numbers for weeks 6-10

■ select each oval shape in turn in cells G17 to K17, so that the oval is enclosed in a selection rectangle. Use the *Delete* key to remove it. Use **Edit-Undo** if you delete the wrong data

■ amend the note at the bottom of the worksheet

■ use the **Format-Cells** menu to remove or change unwanted cell borders.

Weeks 6-10 are reproduced as Appendix 1 – check it with your version. You will see that by the end of week 10 you are £155 in debt. Task 19, 'Testing assumptions', will show you how to try and solve this!

Task 18: Copying a worksheet

We are going to copy the worksheet Sheet1 and then modify the copy.

1 Make sure that the Sheet 1 tab is still selected.

2 Hold down the *Ctrl* key, place the cursor on the Sheet 1 tab and drag with the

mouse. The cursor changes to represent a copy of the worksheet, marked with a '+' sign.

3 Drag the cursor onto the Sheet 2 tab.

4 Release the *mouse button* then the <u>Ctrl</u> key. Excel copies Sheet1, renaming it Sheet1 (2).

5 Click the tab for Sheet1 (2) if necessary. It opens, becoming the active worksheet; it is a replica of Sheet1.

Troubleshooting   If you forgot to hold down the <u>Ctrl</u> key, or released it too soon, then you may have merely moved Sheet1 to a new position rather than copied it. In this case use the mouse to drag it back to its original position and try again.

Task 19: Testing assumptions – what if?

A major advantage of worksheets is the ability to test out various assumptions by altering the values and noting the results – the so-called 'what if' factor. In our example we will find out what would happen if we cut down on the term's expenditure so that we can end the term in the black.

1 Make the following two changes to Sheet1 (2) for weeks 6–10. The easiest way is to amend the relevant value for week 6, then Fill-Right.

   ■ Reduce the amount spent on books to zero.

   ■ Spend £5 less on food and travel per week.

   However you still end the term with a £55 overdraft!

   Save the worksheet at this point.

2 Let's assume that you find a part-time job at £20 a week from week 7 onwards. This involves inserting an extra row to hold this new income category.

   First select the row designator for row 7.

3 Open the **Insert** menu and select **Rows**.

   A new row is inserted, label it **Part Time Job**.

4 Now insert **20** for weeks 7 – 10.

If entered correctly, this extra income means that you end the term with £25.

This is obviously only a simple example of building alternative models, based on different assumptions. In later units we will use more sophisticated analysis tools.

If you are not continuing with the next unit then save and close the workbook.

Summary of commands

Menu commands show the menu name first, followed by the command to choose from the menu, e.g. **Edit-Clear** means open the **Edit** menu and select the **Clear** command.

Edit-Clear-All	Delete cell contents
Edit-Delete	Delete selected rows or columns
Edit-Undo	Undo previous operation
File-Close	Close current workbook
File-Exit	Exit Excel
File-New	Open new, blank workbook
File-Open	Retrieve an existing workbook
File-Page Setup	Amend page settings for printing
File-Print	Print worksheet
File-Save	Save current workbook
Format-Cells-Border	Add cell borders
Format-Column-Width	Adjust column width
Format-Cells-Font	Embolden, italics, character size and style
Format-Cells-Alignment	Align text blocks
Format-Cells-Number	Format numbers, percentages etc.
Format-Row-Height	Adjust row height
Insert-Column	Insert a blank column
Insert-Rows	Insert a blank row
Tools-Options	Do/do not display gridlines etc.
View-Full Screen	Turn on/off full screen mode
Window-Freeze Panes	Freeze row and column headings.
Window-Unfreeze Panes	Unfreeze row and column headings.

Standard Toolbar

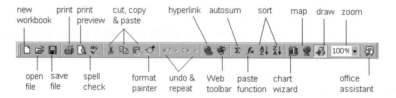

Formatting Toolbar

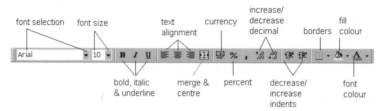

The Drawing Toolbar

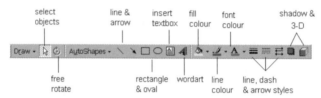

Summary of unit

In this unit you have learned how to

- change the appearance of text by changing font type and size
- align and centre data in cells
- insert and delete columns and rows
- centre the worksheet title
- add borders to the worksheet
- freeze title and labels
- enter and justify blocks of text
- add arrows and shapes to the worksheet
- print a selected section of the worksheet
- add headers and footers
- copy a worksheet
- modify a worksheet.

Other worksheet activities

What you will learn in this unit

By the end of this unit you will be able to

■ name a worksheet

■ delete a worksheet from a workbook

■ use the Excel AutoFormat feature to format worksheets.

What you should know already

Before you start this unit, make sure you can do the following.

Skill	Covered in
Open a workbook and enter simple worksheet data	Units 1 and 2
Edit and delete data	Unit 2
Use the SUM function	Unit 2
Copy a worksheet	Unit 3

What you need

To complete this unit, you will need:

The workbook **TERMS** created in Units 1 – 3.

Introduction

In this unit you will be rounding off your basic worksheet skills and learning how to name and delete worksheets. You will also be using the further Excel formatting features and learning some more simple functions. You will be given the chance to check your progress with some independent work.

Task 1: Naming a worksheet

At the moment our workbook **TERMS** contains two worksheets with the default names Sheet1 and Sheet1 (2). We will give them the more meaningful names **pessimistic model** and **optimistic model**. A sheet name can be up to 31 characters long. It can contain spaces, but the following special characters *cannot* be used: [ ], /, \, ? and *

If you are not continuing from the previous unit then you will need to open the workbook **TERMS** created in Units 1 – 3.

1   Make sure that Sheet1 is selected as the active sheet (click the sheet tab).

2   Open the **Format** menu and select **Sheet**.

3   Select the Rename option. The sheet tab is highlighted.

4   Type the new name *pessimistic model.*

5   Click the OK button. The sheet name appears as the name tab.

6   Repeat this operation for Sheet1 (2), naming it *optimistic model.*

Renaming worksheets makes the name tabs larger. This may mean that not all name tabs are visible at the same time. If so, you will need to use the arrow buttons to the left of the sheet tabs to find the sheet that you need. You can also select the sheet tab for renaming by double-clicking it.

Task 2: Consolidation – check your progress

1   Copy the sheet **'optimistic model'** (hold down the *Ctrl* key and drag the sheet by its tab), renaming it 'Spring Term', then make the following changes to this sheet.

   ■ From week 3 onwards Accommodation rises to £65 a week.

   ■ Your parents send you £30 for your birthday in week 8.

   ■ You want to go to an end-of-term celebration in week 10.

   ■ Modify the value in the **Other** category for week 10 so that you end the Spring Term with £5.

2   Save these changes and use Appendix 2 to check your calculations.

Task 3: Deleting a worksheet from a workbook

From time to time you may need to discard unwanted worksheets from a workbook. We now have three worksheets in the workbook **TERM1.XLS** – **pessimistic model**, **optimistic model**, and **Spring Term**. Let's assume that the first sheet, **pessimistic model** was an original cash flow forecast that is no longer needed.

1   Click the name tab pessimistic model to activate it.

2   Open the **Edit** menu and select the **Delete Sheet** option. A dialog box appears, warning you that the sheet will be permanently deleted.

3   Make sure that you are deleting the correct sheet, then click the OK button.

Task 4: Independent activities

1. Copy the worksheet **Spring Term** (from the **Consolidation** section above) under the new name **Summer Term**.

2. Modify the income and expenditure categories and amounts to fit your own financial situation.

3. Print out the **Summer Term** worksheet using the **File** menu or the **Print** button.

Here are some additional hints on the use of the **Print** options under the **File** menu.

- Use the **Print Area** command to change the print area to include all the worksheet data

- Select **Page Setup** and use the **Page** tab to print width-ways in landscape.

- In the **Print Preview** option check the appearance of your sheet before you print (use the **Zoom** button too).

- Select the **Print** option then the **Active Sheets** option to print the whole sheet.

4   Exit from Excel.

Task 5: Consolidation – averages and percentages

In this section we will recap on some of the skills that you have learnt and also find out how to calculate averages and percentages. We will create a new workbook for this activity.

1   **Calculating totals**. Open a new workbook. If you have started a new Excel session then one is provided, otherwise save and close the present workbook, open the **File** and select **New**.

The **New dialog** box appears.

2   Click the **Workbook** icon then **OK**.

3   Now create the worksheet shown in FIGURE 4.1 as follows.

Format the worksheet as shown

- title centred across columns A – E

- cell labels in bold

- values centred in cells.

4   Now use the *SUM* function to calculate the quarterly totals in cell E4 then copy the formula to cells E5 and E6 using **Edit-Fill-Down** (or the **AutoComplete** button).

5 Calculate the totals in row 9 next using **SUM** and **Edit-Fill-Right**.

Don't just type the totals in.

	A	B	C	D	E
1		Insurance Sales - First Quarter			
2					
3		Motor	Life	Property	Total
4	Jan	1465	1243	2456	
5	Feb	1345	1456	1987	
6	Mar	1132	2310	1598	
7					
8	Quarterly Average				
9	Quarterly Total				
10	% of Total				
11					

FIGURE 4.1

6 Save the worksheet as Workbook **INS_SLS**

■ Remember to select the correct drive.

■ Cancel the Summary Information dialog box if it appears.

7 **Calculating averages**. We now wish to find the average sales for each type of insurance and place them in row 8.

■ Select cell B8 and enter the formula *=AVERAGE(B4:B6)*

■ Click the tick box or press *Enter* and the three cells are averaged (1314).

■ Use **Edit-Fill-Right** to average the **Life, Property** and **Total** categories too.

■ Now centre the row 8 and 9 values in their cells.

■ Use the Format-Cells-Number command to remove the decimal places.

8 Next we will express the quarterly totals – cells B9 to D9 – as fractions of the total sales – cell E9.

■ Select cell B10 and enter the formula *=B9/$E$9*

■ Click the tick box.

The quarterly total for motor insurance is shown as a decimal fraction of the overall quarterly total – the value 0.26294 is displayed in the cell.

Explanation of the formula

■ The / sign represents division.

■ So far all the cell references that you have been using are *relative* references. This means that the references of cells used in a formula are relative to the location of the cell where the formula is placed. In this way the cell references in formulae are automatically adjusted when cells are copied. However this would not work for the percentages that we are calculating as they must all be based upon one fixed cell – E9. We do not want this cell value to be adjusted when we use the **Fill-Right** command. The dollar signs in front of the column and row number make the cell reference into an *absolute* reference and prevent this happening.

You can convert a relative to an absolute reference by selecting the cell formula and pressing the_*F4* function key. Continuing to press it gives combinations of absolute and relative references, known as *mixed* references.

9   **Calculating percentages**. Now to turn this into a percentage.

- Make sure that cell B10 is still selected.

- Open the **Format** menu and select **Cells** then the **Number** tab.

- Click the **Percentage** option in the **Category** box.

- Make sure that the **Decimal Places** box is set to 2 – see FIGURE 4.2.

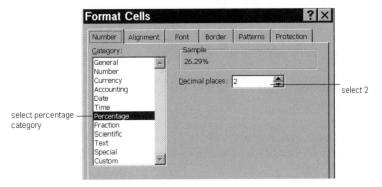

FIGURE 4.2

10 Click **OK**. Motor insurance is now shown as 26.29% of total sales.

11 Use the **Edit-Fill-Right** command to show **Life** and **Property** as percentages too.

Task 6: Adding a text box

Let's add a text box to the worksheet, explaining its function. The Drawing Toolbar is displayed at the bottom of the worksheet – if it is not displayed then open the **View** menu and select the **Toolbars** option.

1   Click the Text Box tool (see the tool bar key at the end of this unit). The pointer changes to cross hairs.

2   Locate the screen pointer on the top left-hand corner of cell B12.

3   Drag across and down to cell E14. The text box is now drawn.

4   Enter the text, ***This worksheet shows a sales analysis of the three major insurance categories.*** You will see that the text wraps automatically to the size of the box.

 Remove an unwanted box by clicking the border to select it. Then select **Clear All** from the **Edit** menu. Make sure that the border of the box is dotted rather than diagonal lines.

5   Compare your worksheet to Appendix 3.

6   Save and close the workbook.

Task 7: Automatic formatting of worksheets

Excel's AutoFormat feature allows you to format your worksheets automatically, offering 17 built-in formats to choose from. Excel will automatically detect which worksheet areas should be headings, data, totals, etc. This allows you to format either a range of cells or a complete worksheet in attractive, standardised formats, thereby saving the time and effort of designing your own.

1   Open the worksheet **INS_SLS.XLS** if necessary.

2   Select all the cells in the worksheet, i.e. cell range A1 to E14.

3   Open the **Format** menu and select **AutoFormat**. A dialog box appears showing a sample worksheet.

Take some time to select each of the various formats listed in the Table format list. The sample worksheet will change to illustrate each format you select.

4   **Selecting a format.** Select the Classic 3 format and then OK . Your worksheet is converted to the format chosen, but you may not be happy with its appearance, e.g. the columns may be too wide.

5   **Undoing a format change.** Open the **Edit** menu and select **Undo AutoFormat** – your worksheet is restored to its previous format.

Edit-Undo will reverse up to 16 previous changes if you keep repeating the command. If this does not work then select **Format-AutoFormat**, then scroll down the **Table Format** list and select the **None** option then OK . You may find, however, that you have lost your original formatting, e.g. bold and centring. If all else fails then closing the worksheet without saving it will undo any disastrous mistakes – but you will also lose any other changes made since the worksheet was opened or saved.

6   **Selecting a sub-format.** Make sure that all the worksheet cells are still selected and open the **AutoFormat** menu again.

   ■ Select the **Classic 3** format from the table.

   ■ Click the Options button.

Six Formats to Apply are offered at the bottom of the dialog box; initially all options are selected. Try deselecting and reselecting all of them and notice their effects on the sample. When a format is deselected, such as Border or Alignment, the present formats continue to apply.

7 **Deselecting a sub-format**. Deselect the Font, Alignment and the Width/Height options then click OK .

The worksheet is reformatted in the Classic 3 format, minus the options that we have deselected.

8 Click the worksheet to remove the selection from the cells.

9 Restore the worksheet to its original format – see Task 4 above.

Task 8: Indenting, rotating and aligning text in cells

1 Select cells A4 to A10.

2 Open the Format menu and select Cells.

3 When the Format Cells dialog box is displayed click the Alignment tab as shown below in FIGURE 4.3.

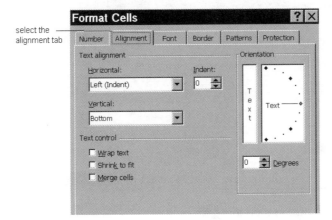

FIGURE 4.3

4 **Indenting text.** Up to 15 indent steps are possible. Increase the indent steps to 2 and click OK – the text is indented.

5 **Rotating text.** Undo the indent using the Edit menu. Make sure that the cells are still selected.

6 Open the Format Cells dialog box again.

This time select 10 in the degrees box.

7 Click OK .

The text is rotated.

8 Undo the rotation using the **Edit** menu.

9 **Aligning text.** Centre the text horizontally and vertically using the dialog box as before.

Task 9: Conditional formatting

Excel 97 allows you to format only those cells whose values lie outside specified limits.

1 Select cell range B4 to **D6.**

2 Open the **Format** menu and select the **Conditional Formatting** option. A dialog box appears. We wish to highlight those cells whose values fall between 1500 and 2000.

3 Complete the dialog box as shown below in FIGURE 4.4.

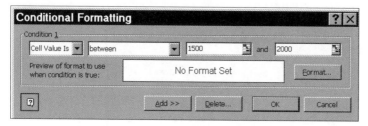

FIGURE 4.4

4 Click the Format button.

When the **Format Cells** dialog box appears select the Border tab.

5 Click the Outline button then the OK button.

You are returned to the **Conditional Formatting** dialog box.

6 Click the OK button. Deselect the cell range and you will see that the cells whose values fall between 1500 and 2000 have a border.

Task 10: Copying formatting

The Format Painter allows us copy Formats quickly. Format the label in cell A4 e.g., to 12 point, bold, colour red – these options are available using the **Format-Cells-Font** menu options.

1 Click the Format Painter button – it is on the Standard Toolbar, marked with a paintbrush – see the key at the end of this unit.

2 Then select another cell or range of cells that you wish to copy this format to, e.g. the column labels in cells A5 and A6.

3   Click the ▓Format Painter▓ button again. The format is copied to these cells, use
    Edit-Undo if it doesn't work correctly.

4   We could choose to save these changes using Save, but we won't bother in this
    instance. Close the workbook without saving.

Summary of commands

Menu commands show the menu name first, followed by the command to choose
from the menu, e.g. Edit-Clear means open the Edit menu and select the Clear
command.

Edit-Clear-All	Delete cell contents
Edit-Delete Sheet	Delete selected worksheet
Edit-Fill-Down	Copy selected cells into selected lower cells
Edit-Fill-Right	Copy selected cells into selected right hand columns
Edit-Undo	Undo previous operation
File-Close	Close current workbook
File-Exit	Exit Excel
File-New	Open new, blank workbook
File-Open	Retrieve an existing workbook
File-Page Setup	Amend page settings for printing
File-Print	Print worksheet
File-Save	Save current workbook
Format-AutoFormat	Apply Excel built-in format
Format-Cells-Number	Format numeric data
Format-Conditional format	Format cells meeting certain conditions
Format-Sheet-Rename	Rename Selected Sheet

Functions

=AVERAGE()	Average range of cells

Standard Toolbar

new workbook   print preview   print   cut, copy & paste   hyperlink   autosum   sort   map   draw   zoom

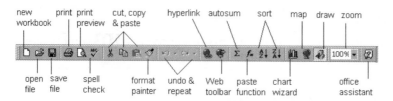

open file   save file   spell check   format painter   undo & repeat   Web toolbar   paste function   chart wizard   office assistant

Formatting Toolbar

font selection   font size   text alignment   currency   increase/ decrease decimal   borders   fill colour

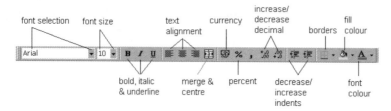

bold, italic & underline   merge & centre   percent   decrease/ increase indents   font colour

The Drawing Toolbar

select objects   line & arrow   insert textbox   fill colour   font colour   shadow & 3-D

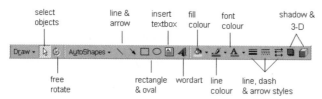

free rotate   rectangle & oval   wordart   line colour   line, dash & arrow styles

Summary of unit

In this unit you have learned how to

- name a worksheet
- delete a worksheet from a workbook
- calculate averages and percentages
- use the **AutoFormat** function
- review, select and undo formats
- select and deselect sub-formats
- indent, rotate and align text in cells
- use the **Conditional Formatting** function
- copy formats.

Creating some simple charts

What you will learn in this unit

By the end of this unit you will be able to

■ create a simple chart using ChartWizard

■ create different types of charts – line graphs, pie charts and bar charts

■ embed a chart in your worksheet

■ create a separate chart sheet.

What you should know already

Skill	Covered in
How to create a simple worksheet	Units 1 and 2

Introduction

In earlier units we covered some important worksheet skills – including entering data, using formulae to calculate and printing. In the next four units we're going to use charts and graphs to present worksheet data in a more visual way. Excel uses a special feature called ChartWizard which guides you through a series of simple steps and lets you create a wide variety of different chart types, line graphs, pie charts, bar charts etc, as well as many sub-types. You can either embed a chart in your worksheet or create it as a separate chart sheet. We will be looking at both approaches and learning how toformat charts for the best results.

Task 1: Creating some chart data

If you are starting a new Excel session then open Excel as before; you will see a blank worksheet window. We need some worksheet data before we can produce charts. Create the following simple worksheet shown in FIGURE 5.1. It shows the number of holidays sold by a travel company for various European countries.

	A	B	C	D	E	F
1	Sunfilled Holidays					
2			Holidays Sold - Europe			
3						
4		1st Quarter	2nd Quarter	3rd Quarter	4th Quarter	Total
5						
6	Italy	85	99	200	93	477
7	Spain	150	246	355	145	896
8	Portugal	120	180	300	123	723
9	Greece	168	277	320	162	927
10	France	70	120	250	110	550
11						
12	Total	593	922	1425	633	3573

FIGURE 5.1

1 Format it as shown, i.e. column widths adjusted and headings and labels in bold.

2 Total the first column in cell B12, using a formula or the AutoSum button.

3 Copy this formula to the next 3 cells. (C12-E12) using **Fill Right** or **AutoFill**.

4 Calculate the totals for cells F6 to F10 in a similar way. As a check calculate the grand total for all holidays – it should be 3573. If not check your data and your formulae!

5 Now save the workbook as ***EUROSLS***.

If the **Summary** dialog box appears enter some information, e.g. title and subject.

We can now use this worksheet to create a variety of charts.

Task 2: Creating a chart using ChartWizard

ChartWizard allows you to create simple charts using the following four steps.

Select the cells you wish to use in the chart, then

- Select the type of chart – bar, column, pie chart, etc.
- Check or change the cells that you wish to chart.
- Specify the chart axis, titles, labels etc.
- Specify whether the chart will be embedded in the worksheet or in its own chart sheet.

These four steps are explained in the four stages below. Dialog boxes guide you through these steps. At each step you have the option of cancelling, getting help, going back a step, or going on to the next step.

ChartWizard Step 1 allows you to select the Chart Type. First we will create a column chart of the first quarter's sales. (Later in this unit, we will look at how to convert this type of chart to a different one.)

1   Select the cell range A6 – B10 (i.e. 10 cells in all).

2   Open the **Insert** menu and select **Chart** (or click the `ChartWizard` button on the Standard Toolbar – see key at the end of this unit). The first **ChartWizard** dialog box is displayed – see FIGURE 5.2.

FIGURE 5.2

Note – Using the Office Assistant

When you call up ChartWizard (and many other Excel dialog boxes) the **Office Assistant** dialog box may be displayed too. If not, click the `Office Assistant` button (marked with a '?') in the bottom left-hand corner of the dialog box. If nothing happens then it may not have been installed. Click 'yes – please provide help'. A further dialog box appears. If you wish, you can keep Office Assistant open to supplement the instructions that follow.

3   Make sure that the `Standard Types` tab is selected.

The default selected at the moment should be Column – check this. Seven sub-types of the column chart are offered. Select each one in turn – an explanation of each type is shown below the chart type.

4   A button asks you to 'Press and hold to view sample'. Do this. A preview of your worksheet data is charted.

5   Finally re-select sub-type 1, the standard column chart.

6   Click the `Next` button to go to ChartWizard Step 2.

7   ChartWizard Step 2 allows you to confirm or change the range of cells (A6-B10) that you wish to chart. First make sure that the `Data Range` tab is selected.

Check the range of cells – notice that they are shown as absolute references – with sheet name and dollar signs inserted, i.e. Sheet1!$A$6:$B$10. If they are incorrect then amend them or press the `Cancel` button and start again.

 You can drag the dialog box to one side by its title bar in order to view the worksheet data better.

8   If correct, click the `Next` button to go to ChartWizard Step 3.

9   ChartWizard Step 3 offers you the option to add titles, legend, data labels, etc. Select the `Titles` tab first.

2   Click the **Chart Title** box and enter ***1st Quarter Holiday Sales***. This is added to the preview box.

10   In the **Category (X) axis** box add the title ***Country***.

11   In the **Value (Y) axis** box add the title ***Number Sold*** – see FIGURE 5.3.

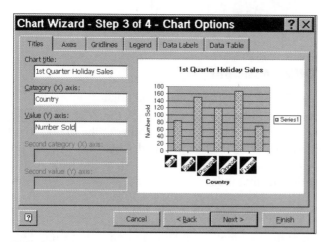

FIGURE 5.3

12   Click the `Legend` tab and deselect the option **Show legend**. The chart will not need one.

The dialog box should now look like FIGURE 5.4.

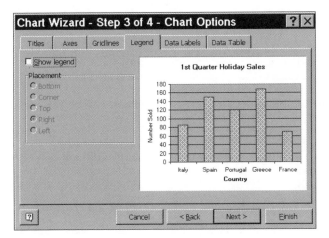

FIGURE 5.4

13   Click the   Next   button to go to ChartWizard Step 4.

14   ChartWizard Step 4 allows you to either embed the chart in the worksheet or display it in its own chart window.

Select the **As New Sheet** option – see FIGURE 5.5.

15   Click the   Finish   button.

The chart is displayed; it is given the default name Chart1 – see the sheet tabs.

FIGURE 5.5

Task 3: Re-sizing the chart

When a chart is first created its size is independent of the window size, with the result that the chart and the titles may be too small. The **View** menu offers two options to resize a chart.

 Don't worry if the Chart Toolbar is displayed – it can be dragged out of the way using its title bar.

1   First maximise the chart window if necessary.

2   Open the **View** menu.

3   Select the option **Sized with Window**. The Chart expands to fill the window space available.

4   Open the **View** menu and select **Full Screen**. The chart can be seen at maximum size.

5   Repeat step 3. The **Sized with Window** option is deselected – it is no longer 'ticked'.

6   Now restore the window size. You will find that part of the chart may no longer be visible.

7   Open the **View** menu and select the **Zoom** option. A dialog box opens allowing you to specify a particular chart size, independent of window size. (This option is unavailable while the **Sized with Window** option is selected.)

8   Try out various scales – the larger the scale the more detail you can read, but the less the amount of the chart that will fit in the window.

9   Try out the **Fit Selection** option on the **Zoom** dialogue box.

    This fits the chart to the window size available.

10 Now open the **View** menu again. Deselect the **Full Screen** option and *re*select the **Sized with Window** option.

The Chart Toolbar

At the moment the Chart Toolbar should be displayed. Normally it appears whenever a chart is displayed. Like other toolbars the purpose of each button is displayed whenever the mouse pointer rests on it. As we will be using ChartWizard and AutoFormat we will turn it off for these activities. It can be turned on again using the View-ToolBars option.

Task 4: Explanation of the chart

Excel has plotted a standard column chart, based on the data contained in cells A6 to B10 of Sheet1 of the workbook **EUROSLS**. Let's study the chart and worksheet for a few moments, and see how Excel plots a chart; key terms that you should remember are in italic.

The five columns on the chart show the values of the five worksheet cells that you selected – cells B6–B10. Rest the mouse pointer on a column and its value is displayed. Each value is called a *data point,* together they form a *data series.* In this simple chart there is one data series – the holidays sold for each country – and five corresponding columns on the chart.

The columns are charted on the *Y* or *vertical* axis, also called the *value* axis.

The *X* or *horizontal* axis shows the five categories; for this reason the X axis is also referred to as the category axis. Excel takes the text labels for each row – Italy, Spain, etc., and places them on the X axis as category names.

Some chart types, e.g. the pie chart, do not use axes. We will be looking at the major chart types in the tasks that follow.

Task 5: Changing the chart type using ChartWizard

Although we have plotted the worksheet data as a column chart, we can convert it to another type of chart using ChartWizard.

1   Make sure that Chart1 and not the worksheet is the active document.

2   Open the **Chart** menu and select **Chart Type**. A dialog box opens, offering you a choice of chart types.

3   Select **Pie** from the **Chart Type** menu. You are offered a choice of several pie chart formats. Format 1 is already selected.

4   Select OK . The chart is re-plotted as a pie chart.

Pie charts are good for showing the relative contributions of various elements to the total 'pie'. This can be shown as a number or as a percentage. However, as there are now no X or Y axes the coloured sections need a key or *legend* to explain them.

Task 6: Adding a legend

1   Open the **Chart** menu and select **Chart Options**.

2   Click the Legend tab.

3   Select **Show Legend** and **Right** from the **Placement** box.

4   Click the OK . button. The legend appears on the chart.

5   Open the **View** menu and check that the **Sized with Window** option is still selected.

Task 7: Moving between chart and worksheet

The pie chart **Chart1** and the worksheet **Sheet1** are two separate documents. At the moment the chart overlays the worksheet – it is the 'active window'. Click the sheet tab for Sheet1 . – it overlays the chart to become the active window.

If the sheet tabs are not visible then maximise the workbook window.

Let's now make the two windows smaller so that we can see chart and worksheet alongside each other – see FIGURE 5.6.

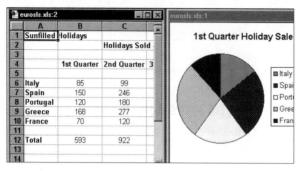

FIGURE 5.6

1   First make that the chart is the active window.

2   Now open the **Window** menu and select the **New Window** option. Excel opens a second window so that more than one workbook document can be seen at the same time.

3   Open the **Window** menu again. Two documents are listed at the bottom of the menu – **EUROSLS.XLS:1** and **EUROSLS.XLS:2**. At the moment they are both copies of the pie chart.

4   Click the sheet tab for Sheet1 to make it the active window.

Task 8: Arranging Windows

Windows offers several ways of viewing both windows at the same time.

1   Open the **Window** menu and select **Arrange**.

     The **Arrange Windows** dialog box appears.

2   Select the **Arrange-Cascade** option.

3   Select the **Windows of Active Workbook** option.

4   Click OK – see FIGURE 5.7.

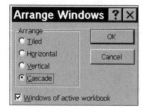

FIGURE 5.7

The two windows are arranged in an overlapping pattern – see FIGURE 5.8 below.

windows overlap
at top left-hand edges

FIGURE 5.8

5   Click on the border of each window. This is a quick way to move from one window to another.

6   Open the **Window/Arrange** menu and option again. This time select the **Arrange Vertical** option (and the **Windows of Active Workbook** option if necessary).

7   Click **OK** . The two windows are displayed side by side – see FIGURE 5.6 above.

8   **Re-sizing the Windows**. Click each window in turn – it becomes the active window and the title bar turns blue. If necessary you can move each window by dragging the title and re-size the chart or the worksheet by dragging the sides. Do not overdo this with the chart as its dimensions can become rather 'squashed'.

9   **Re-sizing chart text**. If you wish to increase the size of the title text double click on it. The **Format Chart Title** dialog box appears, click the **Font** tab and select a different font size.

Troubleshooting Note that sheet tabs are available for both windows. If the chart or the sheet have disappeared check that Sheet1 and Chart1 are the active windows.

Task 9: Re-plotting a chart

Now that Chart and Worksheet are both displayed side by side we can show the dynamic relationship between them.

1   Click the worksheet to activate it.

2   Select cell B7 and amend the number of Spanish holidays to ***500***

3   Press *Enter*. The pie chart also changes to reflect this.

4   Open the **Edit** menu and select **Undo Typing**. The pie chart returns to its previous shape.

5   To close the extra window opened in Task 7, select the worksheet window and click on the **Close** button. Only one window is open now. Maximise it if necessary.

Task 10: Saving and retrieving a chart

1   Open the **File** menu and select **Save**. The chart is saved under its default name *Chart1*, as part of the workbook **EUROSLS.XLS**.

 If you have had several tries at creating charts then the default chart name will be Chart2, Chart3, etc. Deleting an unwanted chart is the same procedure as for a worksheet – Open the **Edit** menu and select **Delete Sheet**.

 Make sure that the correct sheet is selected as the deletion cannot be undone.

2   To check this open the **File** menu and select **Close**.

A dialog box may prompt you to save any changes to Sheet1, the other document in the workbook. If so, click the `Yes` button and exit.

3   Now open the workbook **EUROSLS** again using the **File** menu. You may notice that it is listed at the bottom of the **File** menu. The last four documents that you have used are listed in this way.

Task 11: Moving pie chart segments

1   Make sure that Chart1 is the active sheet in the workbook. Activate the pie chart by clicking it once. Square selection 'handles' appear.

2   Place the screen pointer on the segment denoting Portugal and click once. Handles appear on the segment.

3   Hold down the left mouse button and drag the segment slightly away from the rest of the pie chart – this can be used for emphasis.

4   Press the *Esc* key to turn off the selection handles.

 Use the **Edit-Undo** option to reverse any mistake you make.

 If you double click on the pie then you may call up the **Format Data Point** dialog box. If so cancel the dialog box and try again.

Task 12: Adding values to a chart

It can be difficult to judge the relative proportions of the pie chart segments unless the values are added. The **Chart Options** command allows us to add the actual values to pie segments (and other types of chart).

1   Open the **Chart** menu and select **Chart Options**.

2   Select the `Data Labels` tab.

3   The dialog box offers a number of options – try each one in turn.

4   Select the option **Show Percent** and click OK – see FIGURE 5.9

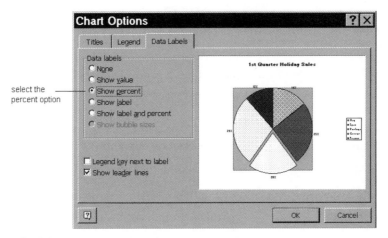

FIGURE 5.9

5   If the percentages are too small then double click on one of them. The **Format Data Labels** dialog box appears.

6   Click the Font tab and select a different font size, e.g. 9 or 10.

Do the same for the legend box. Your pie chart will resemble FIGURE 5.10.

FIGURE 5.10

7   If you are not proceding directly to the next unit then use the **File** menu to save and close your workbook.

Summary of commands

Menu commands show the menu name first, followed by the command to choose from the menu, e.g. **Edit-Clear** means open the **Edit** menu and select the **Clear** command.

Chart-Chart Options	Change title, legend, data labels etc.
Chart-Chart Type	Change the chart type
Edit-Delete Sheet	Delete a chart or worksheet
Edit-Undo Entry	Reverse previous operation
Format-Autoformat	Select pre-formatted chart type
Insert-Chart	Create a new chart
View-Fit Selection	Chart fits window size available
View-Full Screen	Sheet increases to full screen size
View-Zoom	Specify a particular chart size
View-Sized With Window	Re-size chart to window size
Window-Arrange	Arrange layout of windows
Window-New Window	Open extra window

Standard Toolbar

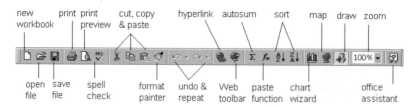

Formatting Toolbar

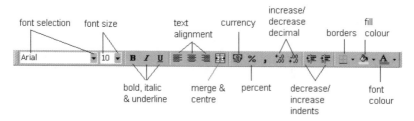

Summary of unit

In this unit you have learned how to

- create a chart using the ChartWizard feature
- resize a chart
- change the chart type using ChartWizard
- add a legend
- move between a chart and a worksheet
- arrange windows
- resize windows
- resize chart text
- replot a chart
- save and retrieve a chart
- move chart segments
- add values to a chart.

Further chart types and skills

What you will learn in this unit

By the end of this unit you will be able to

■ improve the appearance of your charts

■ print charts

■ name and copy charts.

What you should know already

Skill	Covered in
How to create a simple worksheet	Units 1 and 2
How to create a chart	Unit 5

What you will need

To complete this unit you will need

■ the workbook **EUROSLS** created in Unit 5.

Introduction

You now know how to create some simple charts. In this unit we will be learning more on how to alter and improve their appearance and how to print charts. We will also be naming and copying charts.

Task 1: Moving and re-sizing chart items

You may need to alter the size or layout of chart components, e.g. pie segments, title or legend. You can do this quite easily with the mouse – first click the item to select it, then use the appropriate menu or mouse operation. Any item in a chart can be selected in this way. You can also double click or right click a chart component as a shortcut to a menu or a dialog box.

You will find that it takes a little practice to select the right item – particularly when they are close together. Persevere and remember these simple rules.

■ An item is not selected unless it is enclosed in selection 'handles'.

■ Click elsewhere or press the *Esc* key to remove selection handles.

■ Undo an incorrect operation straightaway, using the Edit-Undo option.

■ Single click not double click – if you double click a dialog box will open. Cancel it if this happens.

Note

If you are starting a new Excel session then you will need to open the Workbook **EUROSLS**, created in the previous unit. Make sure that Chart1 is the active sheet.

1 First experiment and click the various parts of the chart in turn to select them – pie segments, segment labels, title and legend.

2 Now click on the **Legend** box.

It is surrounded by a selection rectangle upon which are a number of square 'selection handles' .

3 Move the screen pointer onto the the the top left handle.   The pointer changes to a double-headed arrow and a tip box identifies it – see FIGURE 6.1.

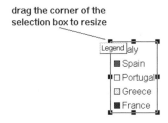

FIGURE 6.1

Drag the selection handle to make the legend slightly larger.

4 Click the outside edge of the pie chart until it is surrounded by a selection rectangle. This can be tricky – make sure that the whole pie is selected not just the individual segments or labels – see FIGURE 6.2.

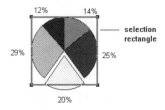

FIGURE 6.2

5 Now make the pie chart slightly larger by dragging the selection handle on the bottom right corner.

Task 2: Moving the title

1 Click the title until it is surrounded by the selection rectangle.

2   Move the mouse pointer onto the edge of the rectangle and drag it up the window.

The title cannot be resized by dragging – see next task for formatting text.

3   Next move the mouse pointer in front of the word 'Holiday' in the title and click. An insertion point is placed there.

4   Insert the word **European**. The title is amended as shown in FIGURE 6.5 below.

Task 3: Changing text fonts and style

We are going to format the pie chart further to improve its appearance. Make sure that the pie chart Chart1 is still the active sheet.

1   First we will make the title more prominent.

Move the screen pointer onto the title and click once. It should be enclosed by a selection rectangle.

2   Open the **Format** menu and select **Selected Chart Title**. The **Format** dialog box appears.

3   Click the Font tab in the dialog box. You are offered a range of fonts, sizes and styles.

4   Choose another font and alter the size to 12 point.

5   Select Bold then OK . The title will now change – press the *Esc* key to deselect it.

Bold and *Italic* options are also available on the Formatting Toolbar.

Task 4: Adding text and arrows

The number of holidays sold for Portugal seems rather low for this quarter, so we'll add a comment to this segment. First check that the Drawing Toolbar is displayed at the bottom of the screen, if not, do step 1 first.

1   Open the **View** menu and select **Toolbars**. The Toolbars list allows you to display further toolbars in addition to the two defaults which are already selected.

2   Select the Drawing toolbar – it is displayed on your chart.

3   Click the arrow button – it is the downwards-pointing arrow – see FIGURE 6.3.

arrow button

FIGURE 6.3

4   The screen pointer changes to a cross; drag to draw the arrow as shown in FIGURE 6.5 below.

If you make a mistake then make sure that the arrow is still selected and press the *Delete* key.

5   Adding text to the arrow is simple. Press the *Esc* key first if necessary to deselect the arrow.

6   Click the Formula Bar at the top of the screen and type the comment **What went wrong?** – see FIGURE 6.4.

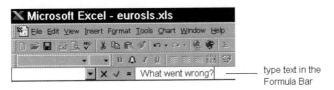

type text in the Formula Bar

FIGURE 6.4

7   Click the Tick Box next to the Formula Bar. The comment now appears on the screen in a text box, enclosed by selection handles.

8   Place the screen pointer on the selection rectangle itself, but not on one of the handles, and drag the box to move it next to the arrow.

9   Now try re-sizing the box by dragging a selection handle. Assuming that the box is still selected, click the **Bold** button.

If you wish to experiment with further styles or colour then use the **Format** menu as you did in Task 3 above. If you have made a serious mistake you can delete selected text with the *Delete* key and start again.

Task 5: Formatting All Chart Text

1   Click the edge of the chart window so that all the chart is selected – small square 'handles' appear around it.

2   Open the **Format** menu and select **Selected Chart Area**. Any formatting options that you select will apply to all the chart elements

3   Using the techniques you have just learnt, format the percentage labels on the pie chart.

If you are happy with the changes – compare your chart with FIGURE 6.5 – then save them, if not use the **Edit-Undo** option.

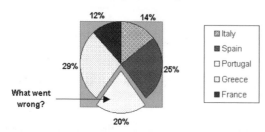

1st Quarter European Holiday Sales

FIGURE 6.5

Task 6: Printing a chart

1 Make sure that Chart1 is the active sheet.

2 Open the **File** menu and select **Print**

You can also use the [Print] button on the Standard Toolbar. A **Print** dialog box opens.

 Troubleshooting If the **Print** option is dimmed it is unavailable, check that you have completed any operations – the tick box should not be displayed in the Formula bar.

3 Select the number of copies – or leave it as the default.

4 Click the [Preview] button.

The Print Preview screen shows the chart as it will appear on the printed page.

 To see more detail, either click the part of the image that you wish to enlarge or use the [Zoom] button at the top of the screen. Press the [Zoom] button again to restore the size.

If you wish to check the page setup or the printer setup then click the buttons at the top of the Print Preview window. If you are satisfied click the [Print] button, otherwise close the dialog box.

If nothing happens then check that

- the printer is switched on – both at the mains and on the printer.
- the Online Switch on the printer is on.
- the cable from the computer to the back of the printer is connected.
- the paper supply/feed trays are OK.

Task 7: Changing chart patterns and colours

If you are using a black and white printer you may find that the coloured segments of the pie chart lack contrast when printed, in which case you can use a pattern rather than a plain block of colour.

1 Make sure that the Chart1 is the active sheet.

2 Click a segment of the pie chart (not the whole chart). The selection handles appear – see FIGURE 6.6.

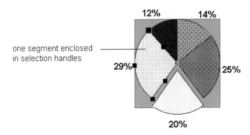

one segment enclosed in selection handles

FIGURE 6.6

3 Open the **Format** menu and select **Selected Data Point**. A dialog box appears.

4 Select the Patterns tab.

This allows you to select:

Border Different edges for the segments

Area Different combinations of colour and pattern for the segments – black and white patterns are best for monochrome printers.

5 Select suitable combinations and click OK .

6 Save the changes to the pie chart.

Task 8: Creating line charts

We are going to use data in the worksheet to create another type of chart – the line chart. Line charts are good for showing trends over time, e.g. comparing sales of two different holidays over four quarters. Each data series is represented by a line on the chart. Each numeric value in the range is shown as a point on the line.

1 Make sure that the workbook **EUROSLS** is open. Make sure that the Sheet1 is the active sheet.

2 Let's compare the sales for Italy and Spain for the four quarters.

Select cells A4 to E7, a range of 20 cells.

3   Open the **Insert** menu and select **Chart**.

The **Chart Wizard 'Step 1 of 4'** dialog box is displayed.

4   Select **Line** from the **Chart** type box.

5   Leave Chart sub-type 4 (the default) selected then click the **Next** button.

6   Make sure that the correct data range, i.e. Sheet1!$A$4:$E$7, is displayed in the **'Step 2 of 4'** dialog box.

7   Click the **Next** button.

As explained in the previous unit, ChartWizard gives both the sheet name as part of the cell range and uses absolute references (the dollar signs).

8   Click the **Next** button on the **'Step 3 of 4'** dialog box.

9   Select the As new sheet option on the **'Step 4 of 4'** dialog box and click the **Finish** button. The line chart appears with the default name Chart2.

10 Open the **View** menu and select the option **Sized with Window**. The line chart expands to fill the window – enlarge the window if necessary. It lacks titles because we did not use ChartWizard to add them; however we can do this at any stage, e.g. in our next task.

Task 9: Adding chart titles and legend

1   Make sure that the line chart created in the previous activity is still the active document.

2   Open the **Chart** menu and select **Chart Options**.

3   Click the **Titles** tab on the *Chart options* dialog box.

4   Enter *Sales for Italy and Spain* in the **Chart Title** box.

5   Add the title *Current Year* to the Category (X) axis box.

6   Similarly in the Value (Y) Axis box type the title *Holidays Sold*.

7   Now click the **Legend** tab to ensure that the **Show Legend** option is selected.

8   Click **OK**.

Task 10: Re-positioning titles and legend using the format menu

You can drag titles and legends to new positions with the mouse but the **Format** menu offers further options which we will try out now. Remember that you can call up the menu directly by right clicking the chart component, or double click it to call up the dialog box.

1 Click the title for the Y axis, ***Holidays Sold*** to select it.

2 Open the **Format** menu and select the option **Selected Axis Title**. The **Format** dialog box opens.

3 Click the **Alignment** tab. You are offered various options. Make sure that horizontal and vertical text alignment are both set to Center – see FIGURE 6.7.

4 Change the text orientation to 0 degrees if necessary.

5 Use the **Font** tab to make the text larger, then click **OK**

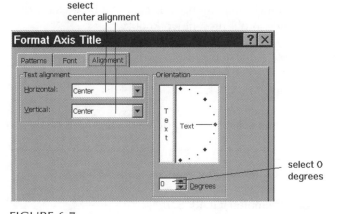

FIGURE 6.7

The title ***Holidays Sold*** is now displayed horizontally – more readably but it may overlap the chart itself. You can select the title then drag it and/or re-size it if this is a problem.

You can see in FIGURE 6.8 that it is also possible to split the title over two lines – see if you can work out how!

Task 11: Independent activities

Using the above operations adjust the font size, style or colour for

■ the X axis title

■ the X and Y axes themselves

■ the legend.

6 Further chart types and skills

Use the **Chart Type** option on the **Chart** menu to try out other Line Chart types – return to sub-type 4 when you have finished.

Finally print the line chart and compare it to FIGURE 6.8.

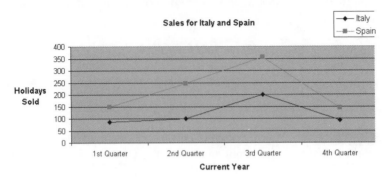

FIGURE 6.8

Task 12: Charting non-adjacent cell ranges

Sometimes you may wish to chart data from different parts of a worksheet. Using the *Ctrl* key we can select cell ranges that are not adjacent and base charts on them, e.g. those for Italy and France in our present workbook.

1 Make sure that the Sheet1 is the active sheet.

2 Select the column headings A4 to E4.

3 Hold down the *Ctrl* key and select the four quarters sales for for Italy – cells A6 to E6.

4 Repeat these operations for the row for France – cells A10 to E10.

The worksheet should resemble FIGURE 6.9.

	A	B	C	D	E	F
1	Sunfilled Holidays					
2			Holidays Sold - Europe			
3						
4		1st Quarter	2nd Quarter	3rd Quarter	4th Quarter	Total
5						
6	Italy	85	99	200	93	477
7	Spain	150	246	355	145	896
8	Portugal	120	180	300	123	723
9	Greece	168	277	320	162	927
10	France	70	120	250	110	550
11						
12	Total	593	922	1425	2940	3573

FIGURE 6.9

5 Now create another line chart on a new sheet, using ChartWizard as before, adding a legend. Your chart should resemble FIGURE 6.10.

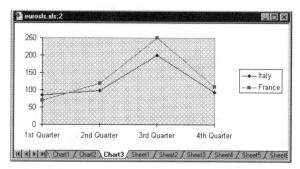

FIGURE 6.10

6   Add suitable titles to the chart and format the text – see previous tasks. This chart
    has the default name Chart3 (or a later number if you have created other charts).

Task 13: Naming charts

At the moment the workbook **EUROSLS.XLS** contains a worksheet with the default
name Sheet1, plus three charts with the default names:

Chart1 – the pie chart created in Unit 5.

Chart2 – the line chart (Italy and Spain) created in Task 7 in this unit.

Chart 3 – the line chart (Italy and France) created in Task 10 in this unit.

Your documents may be numbered differently, depending on how many other sheets
and charts you have created. We will give them more meaningful names. A chart
name, like a sheet name, can be up to 31 characters long. It can contain spaces, but
the following special characters cannot be used: [ ], /, \, ? and *

1   Make sure that Sheet1 is the active sheet – the sheet tab should be selected.

If the sheet tabs are not visible then you may need to maximise the document
window.

2   Open the **Format** menu and select **Sheet** then the **Rename** options (or simply
    double click on the sheet name tab). The name on the tab is selected.

3   Type the name *Euro Hols Data*.

4   Repeat these steps for the three charts.

    ■ Activate the other chart sheets in turn.

    ■ Name the pie chart PIE1 and the line charts LINE1 and LINE2 respectively.

    The sheet tabs at the bottom of the screen should now resemble FIGURE 6.11.

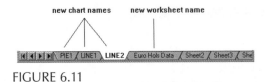

new chart names   new worksheet name

FIGURE 6.11

Task 14: Copying a chart under a new name

Excel allows you to copy a sheet under a new name. We will do this and then modify the copy, leaving the original unchanged.

1   Click the name tab for **Line2** to make it the active window.

2   Hold down the *Ctrl* key and then use the mouse pointer to drag the name tab along past the next name tab. The cursor changes to an icon marked with a + sign. The place where the copy will be placed is marked with a small triangle.

3   First release the mouse button *then* the *Ctrl* key. The copy is made – the name tab is marked **LINE2** (2).

Troubleshooting If you let go the *Ctrl* key too soon then you may merely have moved **Line2** to a new position. In this case use the mouse on the name tab to drag it back to its original position and try again.

4   Now use the **Format** menu as before to rename the copy **LINE3**. If you are not proceding directly to the next unit then use the **File** menu to save and close your workbook.

Summary of commands

Menu commands show the menu name first, followed by the command to choose from the menu, e.g. **Edit-Clear** means open the **Edit** menu and select the **Clear** command.

Chart-Chart Options	Change title, legend, data labels etc.
File-Print	Print Chart
Format-Selected	Format selected chart element
Format-Sheet-Rename	Name a chart sheet
Insert-Chart	Create a new chart
View-Sized with Window	Re-size chart to size of window
View-Toolbars	Show or hide a toolbar

Summary of unit

In this unit you have learned how to

- move and resize chart items
- move the chart title
- format a chart
- print a chart
- change chart patterns and colours
- create line charts
- add chart titles and legend
- reposition titles and legend using the **Format** menu
- chart non-adjacent cell ranges
- name a chart
- copy a chart under a new name.

Further chart operations

What you will learn in this unit

By the end of this unit you will be able to

- rescale a chart axis
- delete a chart
- create an area chart
- add and remove chart values
- reverse chart axes
- add and remove gridlines
- produce bar and column charts
- add trendlines
- change chart values using the Goal Seek feature
- create embedded charts as part of a worksheet.

What you should know already

Skill	Covered in
How to create a simple worksheet	Units 1 and 2
How to create a chart	Unit 5

What you will need

To complete this unit you will need

- the workbook **EUROSLS** created in Unit 5.

Introduction

In this unit we look at chart axes and chart values in more detail. We also create bar, column and area charts.

Task 1: Re-scaling a chart axis

On the line chart LINE2 (and the copy LINE3) the values for Italy and France are very close at some points, making them difficult to read. This is because the scale is not the best one for the range of values on the chart. We can change this default scale.

 If you are starting a new Excel session then you will need to open the workbook **EUROSLS**.

1 Make sure that **LINE3** is the active window.

2 Move the screen pointer onto the vertical axis and click it to select it. Selection handles appear at both ends of the axis.

3 Open the **Format** menu and select **Selected Axis**. A dialog box appears.

4 Select the **Scale** tab. The dialog box now resembles FIGURE 7.1.

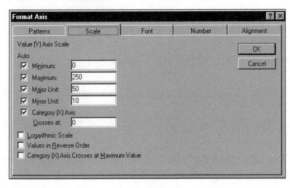

FIGURE 7.1

The axes and scales on charts are calculated automatically – hence the check marks in the Auto boxes – from 0 to 250, the minimum and maximum values.

5 Type **50** in the Minimum box and click **OK**.

The chart is replotted to show the new range from 50 to 250, the scale is also plotted in smaller divisions, making values easier to compare.

6 Open the **Edit** menu and choose the **Undo** and **Re-do** commands to review this.

7 Open the **File** menu and select **Save** to save the changes.

Task 2: Deleting a chart

Let's assume that you wish to use the re-scaled chart **LINE3** and discard **LINE2**. You can delete this chart from the workbook

1 Click the name tab for **LINE2** – check that it is now the active chart.

2 Open the **Edit** menu and select the **Delete Sheet** option.

3   A dialog box warns you that the sheet will be permanently deleted.

4   Check that the correct sheet is selected then click **OK** . The sheet is now deleted – check that the name tab has disappeared.

 Troubleshooting   If you have deleted the wrong sheet there is still a last resort – exiting Excel *without* saving your work. Assuming that you save your work regularly then not too much work will be lost.

Task 3: Creating area charts

So far we've covered column, pie and line charts. Area charts show both the amount of change over time, plus the sum of these changes. For example, in the case of European holidays we are not only interested in the performance for each country, but its individual contribution to the total holidays sold. Essentially, an area chart is a series of line charts stacked on top of each other with the areas between shaded in.

1   Make the worksheet **Euro Hols Data** the active window.

2   Select cells A4 to E10, i.e. all countries, all quarters.

3   Create a new chart as before using ChartWizard, selecting Area as the chart type.

There are a number to choose from, try them all using the **Sample** button on Step1 of ChartWizard.

Note – Using the Office Assistant

When you call up ChartWizard (and many other Excel dialog boxes) the Office Assistant dialog box may be displayed too. If not click the **Office Assistant** button (marked with a ' **?** ') in the bottom left-hand corner of the dialog box. If nothing happens then it may not have been installed. Take the 'Help with this feature' option. A further dialog box appears, click the button offering you an example of the selected chart type. If you wish you can keep Office Assistant open to supplement the instructions that follow.

4   Now select area chart sub-type 2.

5   When you get to Step3 of ChartWizard select the **Data Labels** tab.

6   Select the **Show Label** option.

7   At Step4 of ChartWizard, select the **As New Sheet** option.

8   When you finish ChartWizard use the **View-Sized with Window** option to enlarge the chart to the size of the window.

9 Using the **Chart-Chart Options** command add a suitable title to the chart – see FIGURE 7.2.

Task 4: Formatting all chart text

1 Click the edge of the chart window so that all the chart is selected.

 Small square 'handles' appear around it.

2 Open the **Format** menu and select **Selected Chart Area**.

3 Select the ▐**Font**▐ tab and change the fonts to 9 point bold.

FIGURE 7.2

4 Name the chart **AREA1** using the **Format-Sheet-Rename** command.

5 Finally delete the legend (select it and use the *Delete* key).

Task 5: Removing chart values

You can remove a range of values from a chart without needing to re-plot it; it is simply a matter of selecting that part of the chart and deleting it. Conversely you can add a range of values to a chart simply by copying and pasting from the worksheet to the chart.

1 Make sure that AREA1 is the active chart.

2 Click once on the area for the third quarter, (not on the name). It should now have a number of selection handles; the formula for the cell range is confirmed in the **Formula Box** at the top of the window – see FIGURE 7.3.

The formula looks more complex than it really is because for each cell in the range plotted – D4 to D10 – Excel includes both the sheet name **Euro Hols Data** and the $ symbol, indicating an absolute reference.

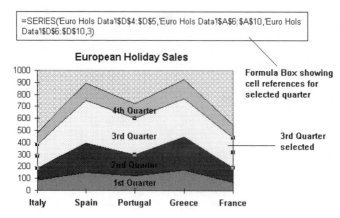

=SERIES('Euro Hols Data'!$D$4:$D$5,'Euro Hols Data'!$A$6:$A$10,'Euro Hols Data'!$D$6:$D$10,3)

European Holiday Sales

Formula Box showing
cell references for
selected quarter

4th Quarter

3rd Quarter

3rd Quarter
selected

2nd Quarter

1st Quarter

Italy   Spain   Portugal   Greece   France

FIGURE 7.3

Make sure that you select the whole area, not the area label; press the *Esc* key to deselect – or simply click the correct part of the chart.

Double clicking calls up a dialog box – simply click the **Cancel** button.

3   Now press the *Delete* key. Quarter 3 is removed (the **Edit-Undo Clear** command will reverse it if you make a mistake).

Task 6: Adding values to a chart

1   Click the name tab for the worksheet **Euro Hols Data** to make it the active window.

2   Select the cell range D4 – D10, i.e. for the third quarter that we have just removed.

3   Open the **Edit** menu and select **Copy**.

4   Now make Area1 the active window again.

5   Open the **Edit** window and select **Paste**. The range of values for the third quarter is pasted back into the chart, but in an incorrect position.

Task 7: Changing the position of a data series

1   Click the third quarter area of the chart again so that it is selected – enclosed in selection handles.

2   Open the **Format** menu and select the option **Selected Data Series**.

3   When the **Format Data Series** dialog box appears, click the **Series Order** tab. The dialog box allows you to select the third Quarter and move it to its correct position.

4   Do this, then click **OK** . The third Quarter is now restored to its correct position – compare it to FIGURE 7.3 above.

 You may need to re-size the window.

Task 8: Reversing the chart axes

Study the chart AREA1 carefully; it shows the five countries as the categories (along the X or category axis) and the holidays sold in each quarter as the values (along the Y or value axis). However it could be equally useful if the axes were reversed, i.e. if each quarter formed the categories along the X axis, and the number of holidays the values on the Y axis. When it plots a chart Excel assumes that you want fewer data series than categories as this is easier to read. In the worksheet **Euro Hols Data** five rows and four columns of data were charted, (excluding cell labels) so the columns B to E become the values plotted and the rows 6 to 10 the categories. We can reverse this using ChartWizard, either by creating a new chart or by modifying an existing one.

1   Make sure that **AREA1** is the active sheet.

2   Click the **ChartWizard** button on the Standard Toolbar – see key at the end of this unit. The **ChartWizard** dialog box appears – notice that it is labelled 'Step 1 of 4'.

3   Check that Area Chart sub-type 2 is still selected. Click the **Next** button.

ChartWizard – Step 2 is displayed next; make sure that the Series tab is selected. Look at the Category (x) axis labels of the dialog box. At the moment the x axis is based on cells A6–A10 of the **Euro Hols Data** workbook, which contain the names of the countries. The formula presently displayed, ='Euro Hols Data'!$A$6:$A$10 reflects this.

!$A$6:$A$10 are the cells – the dollar signs indicate an absolute reference and are optional.

='Euro Hols Data'! is the name of the worksheet upon which the chart is based – the formula requires that it is enclosed in single quotes and that it is separated from the cell references by an exclamation mark.

4   Amend this reference to *='Euro Hols Data'!b4:e4* – see FIGURE 7.4 below.

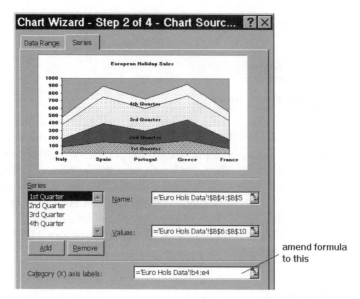

FIGURE 7.4

5 Click the **Data Range** tab now and enter the formula *='Euro Hols Data'!a4:e10* in the **Data range** box – see FIGURE 7.5. (The entire chart is based on cell range A4 to E10.)

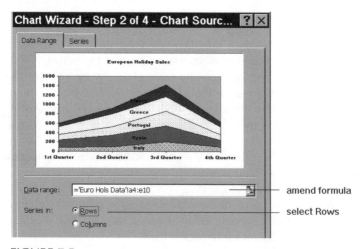

FIGURE 7.5

6 Click the **Rows** button. The chart axes are reversed.

7 Click the **Finish** button.

We can have in effect two views of the same data.

Data series in columns – the countries are the categories, the values for the quarters are plotted on the value axis – see FIGURE 7.2 above.

Data series in rows – the quarters are categories , the values for the countries are plotted on the value axis – see FIGURE 7.6 below – some of the chart patterns have been changed for visibility.

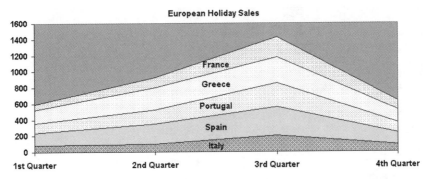

FIGURE 7.6

These techniques can be applied to other chart types.

8 **Independent activity**. Try reversing these changes, showing the data series in columns again – see FIGURE 7.2 above.

Task 9: Adding and removing gridlines

Often ChartWizard provides gridlines to a chart by default – they can help us to read off the values more clearly.

1 Make sure that the chart AREA1 is the active window.

2 Open the **Chart** menu and select **Chart Options**.

3 Select the **Gridlines** tab.

4 Select and deselect the gridlines options for both the Category Axis and the Value Axis and note the effects.

  Gridlines can be deleted or modified at any time using the above steps.

5 Close the **EUROSLS** workbook.

Task 10: Bar charts and column charts

Bar charts show data values as a series of horizontal bars, column charts show values as vertical columns. A bar or column on a chart represents a single number on the worksheet. Both are suited to showing the relative sizes of two or more items; column charts are often used for showing change over time, bar charts are often used to compare the sizes of items at one point in time.

1 To produce these charts we're going to use another worksheet – see FIGURE 7.7. Create it in a new workbook.

2 Open the **File** menu and select **New**.

3 Save it as **BOOKSLS**.

	A	B	C	D	E
1		Book Sales - Current Year			
2					
3	Month	No. Sold	Revenue	Advertising	
4	Jan	850	2011	300	
5	Feb	1010	3155	425	
6	Mar	1175	3550	500	
7	Apr	1430	4536	750	
8	May	1710	5150	800	
9					

FIGURE 7.7

4 Select cells A3 – D6 and create a new chart as follows.

5 Open the **Insert** menu and select **Chart**.

6 Follow the ChartWizard steps as before, selecting bar chart, sub-type 1 as a new sheet.

7 Open the **View** menu and select **Sized with Window**.

If the text labels are too small then click the whole chart area to select it (see Task 4).

Open the **Format** menu and choose **Selected Chart Area**.

Click the **Font** tab and select Bold, Size 9.

The chart produced is the standard clustered bar chart, showing each month's values as a separate set of bars – see FIGURE 7.8.

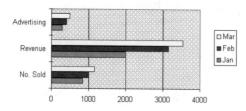

FIGURE 7.8

8 Name the bar chart **BAR1** (double click the sheet tab).

Return to the worksheet Sheet1 and, making sure that cells A3 to D6 are still selected, create a second bar chart as a new chart. This time select the second sub-type of bar chart – stacked bars. The third sub-type, the 100% stacked bar is also useful – it shows the values as percentages. Review this if you like.

9 Open the **View** menu and select Sized with Window.

10   Format the text labels as before if necessary.

12   Save it as **BAR2** – see FIGURE 7.9.

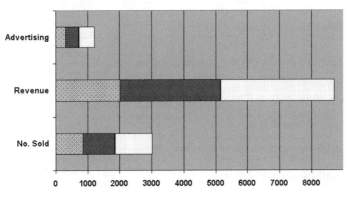

FIGURE 7.9

Each bar is the sum of the three smaller bars. This allows us to see the contribution of each month to the three months total for revenue, sales and advertising.

Task 11: Independent activity – column charts

1   Return to the worksheet and make sure that cells A3 to D8 are selected. Use ChartWizard to experiment with different types of column chart.

Try to produce the column chart shown in FIGURE 7.10 – you will need to reverse the axes in order to show the five months as the values on the Y axis and **Sold, Advertising** and **Revenue** as categories on the X axis (see Task 8).

2   Open the View menu and select Sized with Window.

3   Format the text labels as before if necessary.

4   Save the sheet as **COLUMN1**.

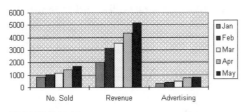

FIGURE 7.10

Task 12: Adding trendlines

1   Make sure that worksheet Sheet1 in the workbook **BOOKSLS** is the active window.

2   Make sure that cells A3 to D8 are selected.

3 Use ChartWizard to create a standard column chart as a new sheet. This time accept the default axis settings so that the months are the categories on the X axis.

4 Open the **View** menu and select **Sized with Window**.

5 Format the text labels as before if necessary (see Task 4).

6 Move the screen pointer onto one of the bars representing advertising and click. All five bars representing advertising are selected.

7 Open the **Chart** menu and select **Add Trendline**.

   The **Add Trendline** dialog box appears.

8 Click the **Type** tab.

9 Select **Linear** then the **Advertising** series. Click **OK**. A trendline is added to the chart – see FIGURE 7.11.

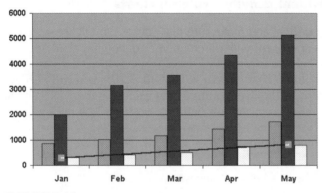

FIGURE 7.11

The trendline is useful for emphasising relationships between different data series – in this case the correlation between advertising, sales and revenue. Sales and revenue are still rising whilst the money spent on advertising has started to level off.

10 Name the sheet **Trend1**.

11 Experiment with the other trendlines offered.

12 Save and close the workbook.

Task 13: Using Goal Seek

Just as you can change values in a chart by amending the underlying worksheet data you can also drag the data points in a chart and change the values on the worksheet. If the changed values are derived from other values via worksheet formulae then these will change too.

1   Open the workbook **EUROSLS**.

2   Make **Euro Hols Data** the active sheet.

3   Make sure that cells A12 to F12 containing the overall totals are selected.

4   Use ChartWizard to create a standard column chart as a new sheet. Accept the default axis settings so that the months are the categories on the X axis.

5   Open the **View** menu and select **Sized with Window**.

   6   Format the text labels as before if necessary (see Task 4).

7   Name the sheet **Goal Seek**.

8   Move the screen pointer onto the fifth (grand total) column and click once, then click again. The column should now be selected – enclosed in selection handles.

9   Now move the pointer onto the top of the bar. The pointer should change to a double-headed arrow. An information box should also open.

10   Now drag the column upwards until its value equals 4000.

A **goal seek** dialog box opens – see FIGURE 7.12 – and the worksheet is displayed.

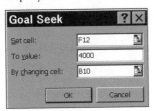

FIGURE 7.12

We can now modify any of the cell range B6 to E10 to achieve the sales goal of 4000 holidays sold.

11   Complete the dialog box as shown above and click **OK**. The value of cell B10 is changed to 497 – the number of French holidays sold to achieve the goal of 4000 in cell F12.

12   Click the **Cancel** button on the dialog box now; this restores the cells to their previous values.

13   Save and close the workbook.

Notes on Goal Seek

The Goal Seek Status dialog box displays two extra buttons.

■ **Pause** – allows you to pause during goal seeking

■ **Step** – allows you to continue one step at a time.

Goal seeking will only work if the cell whose value you set contains a value, not a formula. The cell whose value you set must be related by a formula to the cell whose target value you are changing.

You can also Goal Seek in a worksheet – see Unit 11, Task 1.

Task 11: Consolidation – check your progress

This task gives you the chance to try out some additional techniques and briefly reviews some Excel charts and techniques that we have not yet covered.

1   Open the workbook **EUROSLS**.

2   Open the worksheet **Euro Hols Data**.

3   Create a 3-D stacked area chart showing holidays sold for Italy, Spain and Portugal for all four quarters. Use the ChartWizard techniques used in previous tasks.

4   Modify the chart as follows so that it resembles FIGURE 7.13.

Name the chart **3-D AREA.**

■ Add titles.

■ Embolden the chart text.

■ Alter the patterns of the three areas.

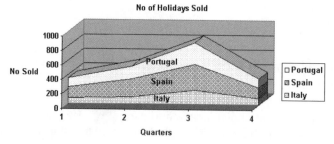

FIGURE 7.13

5   Open the workbook **BOOKSLS**.

6   Add a further column (E) to the worksheet, using formulae to show advertising as a percentage of revenue for each month – see FIGURE 7.14

	A	B	C	D	E
1			Book Sales - Current Year		
2					
3	Month	No. Sold	Revenue	Advertising	As % of Revenue
4	Jan	850	2011	300	15%
5	Feb	1010	3155	425	13%
6	Mar	1175	3550	500	14%
7	Apr	1430	4356	750	17%
8	May	1710	5150	800	16%
9					

FIGURE 7.14

7 Use the column E percentages to create a line chart; name the chart **LINE 1**. It should resemble the chart shown below – FIGURE 7.15.

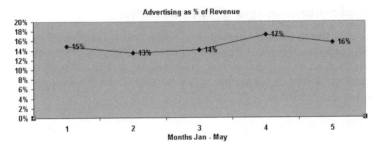

FIGURE 7.15

■ Add titles and axis labels as shown.

■ Embolden the text.

■ Remove the gridlines (Chart-Chart Options).

8 ■ Open the **Chart** menu.

■ Select the Add Trendline option.

■ Add a linear trendline that forecasts forward for a month.

■ Use the Chart-Chart Options menu to show the data table on which the chart is based.

Task 15: Creating a doughnut chart

A doughnut chart is like a pie chart; it shows the relative contribution of various quantities to a total. However unlike a pie chart it is not restricted to one data series.

1 Open the workbook **BOOKSLS**.

2 Highlight cell range A3 to C6 in Sheet1 – the columns showing revenue and number sold for January to March.

3 Using ChartWizard create the doughnut chart shown in FIGURE 7.16.

4 Name the chart **Doughnut1**.

105

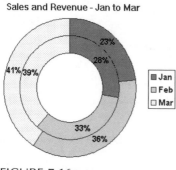

Sales and Revenue - Jan to Mar

FIGURE 7.16

Task 16: Adding arrows and shapes to a chart

It is not clear that the outer ring on the chart represents revenue and the inner ring sales. Let's add notes to the chart to clarify this – see FIGURE 7.17 below.

1 If the Drawing toolbar is not visible at the bottom of the screen open the **View** menu and select **Toolbars**.

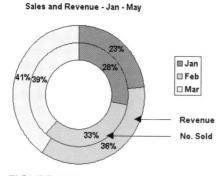

Sales and Revenue - Jan - May

FIGURE 7.17

2 Use the textbox and the arrow tools to create the labels shown. You can delete a selected object by pressing the *Delete* key.

Custom charts

Step 1 of ChartWizard offers a range of custom charts as a separate tabbed sheet 'Custom Types'. Open ChartWizard and take time to review them. Many are just more showy versions of chart types that we have already used, e.g. 'Blue Pie' and 'Colored Lines'. Others offer monochrome versions of standard charts, useful if you don't have a colour printer. Some offer alternative ways of presenting data, e.g. 'Logarithmic' or 'Lines on 2 Axes'.

3 Save and close the workbook **BOOKSLS**.

Task 17: Embedded charts

So far we have created separate chart documents. Excel also allows us to create embedded charts which form part of the worksheet. It is simply a matter of selecting the option at Step 4 of ChartWizard. This is useful if you want to view or print a chart and worksheet on the same page.

1   Open the worksheet **INS_SLS**.

2   Maximise the worksheet window.

3   Highlight the cell range A3 to D6.

4   Open ChartWizard and create a standard bar chart.

5   When you reach Step 4, leave the option as object in selected and press the **Finish** button. The embedded chart is created – see FIGURE 7.18; it can be moved or re-sized using the selection handles. Chart and worksheet can be selected in turn by clicking.

Notice that when one of the bars on the chart is selected Excel's Range Finder will outline the corresponding worksheet elements.

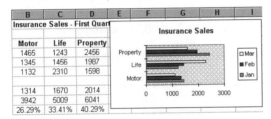

FIGURE 7.18

Task 18: Drag and drop

This is a feature of all Excel's charts and worksheets; it allows you to select a cell range and drag it directly onto a chart to create a new data series. It is especially useful for an embedded chart. We can add the quarterly average figures to the chart in this way.

1   Select cell range A8 to D8 on the worksheet.

2   Move the mouse pointer onto the edge of the selected range. See FIGURE 7.19.

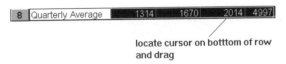

locate cursor on botttom of row
and drag

FIGURE 7.19

3   Now use the mouse to drag the cell range (represented by a dotted rectangle) onto the chart. The chart is re-drawn to include a fourth data series.

 Use the **Edit-Undo** command if you have made a mistake.

To format the embedded chart double click it. The dialog box will be displayed and the chart can be formatted as if it were a separate document.

A chart can be deleted – select it and press the *Delete* key.

You can save or print the chart now as part of the worksheet.

To view the embedded chart in its own window make sure that it is still selected. Then open the **View** menu and select **Chart Window**.

To view the chart as a separate sheet open ChartWizard again. When you reach Step 4 select the option as new sheet option then click the █Finish█ button.

4   Exit from Excel, saving any changes.

Summary of commands

Menu commands show the menu name first, followed by the command to choose from the menu, e.g. **Edit-Clear** means open the **Edit** menu and select the **Clear** command.

Chart-Chart Options	Change title, legend, data labels etc
Chart-Add Trendline	Add a trendline to selected chart data
Edit-Copy...Paste	Copy data from worksheet to chart
Edit-Delete Sheet	Delete a chart sheet
Edit-Undo/Redo	Undo/redo a change to a chart
File-New	Create new workbook
File-Save	Save workbook
Format-Selected	Format selected chart element
Insert-Chart	Create a new chart
Insert-Chart-On This Sheet	Create an embedded chart
Insert-Titles	Insert chart or axis title
View-Sized With Window	Re-size chart to window size

Standard Toolbar

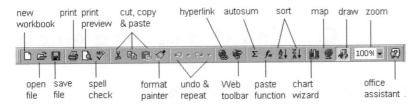

Formatting Toolbar

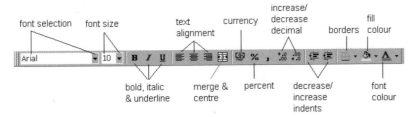

Summary of unit

In this unit, you have learned how to

- rescale a chart axis
- delete a chart
- create an area chart
- format all chart text
- add and remove chart values
- reverse chart axes
- add and remove gridlines
- create bar and column charts
- add trendlines
- use Goal Seek to change chart values
- create a doughnut chart
- add arrows and shapes to a doughnut chart
- create embedded charts within a worksheet
- create a new data series using the Drag and Drop feature.

Creating and using a database

What you will learn in this unit

By the end of this unit you will be able to

■ plan and build a simple database

■ sort a database

■ create new fields

■ maintain a database using a Data Form

■ add subtotals to a database

■ search the database using AutoFilter.

What you should know already

Skill	Covered in
How to start Excel	Unit 1
Basic mouse, menu and Windows operations	Unit 1
How to create a simple worksheet	Unit 2

Introduction

In previous units we have covered worksheets and charts, the first two components of Excel. This unit covers the third component, databases. Businesses use databases to store and retrieve records of all types – customers, employees, goods in stock, etc. FIGURE 8.1 is an example of a simple database that records customer orders. We can use it to introduce certain key database terms.

	A	B	C	D	E
1	Order No.	Order Date	Co.Ref	Co. Name	Value
2	14000	10-Mar	1453	Wilson Garages	3200.00
3	14001	08-Mar	2413	Patel Industries	1466.00
4	14002	11-Mar	1453	Wilson Garages	98.76
5	14003	11-Mar	1289	Marsden Products	4456.00
6	14004	10-Mar	2413	Patel Industries	567.00
7	14005	11-Mar	955	Tilley Transport	1678.00
8	14006	10-Mar	2375	Patel Kitchens	55.54
9	14007	09-Mar	1453	Wilson Garages	2654.00
10	14008	12-Mar	2245	Goldfield Stables	123.85
11	14009	12-Mar	1289	Marsden Products	1652.54
12					

FIGURE 8.1

Record   There is an entry for each order. Each entry is called a *record* and takes up a row.

 Field   Each record contains the same five *fields* or items of information – **Order No, Order Date**, **Co. Ref**, **Co. Name** and **Value.** Each field takes up a column. The first row of the database contains the *field names*, the other rows contain the actual data – the field *values.*

Database   At the moment our database consists of a range of ten records.

Excel is primarily a spreadsheet and does not offer all the features of a special-purpose database management system such as Access or Paradox, but you can perform straightforward database tasks such as

■ finding individual records

■ adding and deleting records

■ editing existing records

■ sorting records.

More complex tasks are also possible, such as sorting records into a different order, or extracting all records meeting a particular search criterion.

Database rules in Excel

Database size   A database can be as large as the entire worksheet, but cannot occupy more than one worksheet. A worksheet can hold several databases.

Fields/Field names   A database can contain up to 256 fields. The first row of the database must contain the field names. Field names must consist of letters only, not numbers, blank cells, etc. Field names can be up to 256 characters long and must be unique

Records   A database can contain up to 16,383 records. Every record must have the same fields, but fields can be left blank. Do not enter extra blanks at the start of fields.

Capitalisation   Excel ignores upper or lower case when searching or sorting the database, so you may use either, e.g.'SMITH', 'smith' or 'Smith' to locate a record.

Building the database

It is essential to plan the structure of a database before you create it. The information that you need will determine what fields you include. For example, FIGURE 8.1 above shows a database set up to keep track of customer orders. We therefore need to know not only the customer details – name and reference code – but also the order details – date, reference code and value. Each of these information items is given its own field and can be processed separately. Notice that we also have implicitly decided what *not* to store, e.g. the customer address – this would probably be stored in a customer database rather than an orders database.

Task 1: Inserting the field names

1   First open a new blank workbook.

2   Enter the five field names shown shown in FIGURE 8.1. (cells A1 – E1)

3   Use the right arrow key to move across the columns.

4   Widen the columns where necessary, and centre and embolden the field names.

Task 2: Entering data using AutoComplete

1   First complete columns C and D – the Co. Ref and Co. Name fields as shown in FIGURE 8.1.

   You may notice that when you enter a company name for the second time, e.g. Wilson Garages, Excel automatically completes the entry for you. Excel keeps a track of duplicated entries and automatically finishes it for you after one or two letters have been entered. You can stop typing and go on to the next cell entry. As there are two companies starting with 'Patel' you will need to type in the rest of the company name.

 The AutoComplete feature can be set on or off. Open the Tools menu and select Options. A dialog box appears. Click the **Edit** tab and select the option 'Enable AutoComplete for Cell Values'.

2   Next enter the order values in column E, the **Value** field. Don't enter .00 after a value if there are no pence. So, for example, in the case of cell E3 just enter *1466* as the value.

Task 3: Formatting the fields

Now we will format the values to 2 decimal places.

1   Select the 10 value fields – cell range E2 to E11.

2   Open the **Format** menu and select the **Cells** option.

   A dialog box appears.

3   Click the **Number** tab and then the **Number** category if necessary.

4   Select 2 from the **Decimal places** list and click the **OK** button – see FIGURE 8.2.

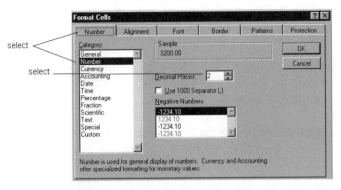

FIGURE 8.2

Task 4: Creating a data series

The **Order No.** field is a numeric sequence – increasing by 1 for every new order record. We can use the **Fill Series** command when numbers or dates in adjacent cells increase (or decrease) by a constant factor.

1 Enter the start value **14000** in cell A2.

2 Select the whole range, A2 to A11.

3 Open the **Edit** menu. Select the **Fill** option then the **Series** option. A dialog box appears, make sure that the following options are selected, as shown in FIGURE 8.3.

FIGURE 8.3

Series in:

Columns   the data series will occupy a column

Linear   the progression will be linear

Step value 1   the numbers will increase by 1 each time (for weekly dates you would step value 7).

4 Click the **OK** button. The column is filled with the order numbers 14000-14009.

You can create a data series based on dates and fractional numbers too.

Task 5: Entering the order date

Excel allows dates to be entered in a variety of formats and in most cases will automatically assign the correct date format.

113

1 Enter the first date field as *10mar* and press *Enter*. Excel automatically converts it to the date format **10-Mar** (if it doesn't then check what you have entered).

2 Enter the remaining field values in a similar way. Look at the status bar at the top of the screen as you do this. Irrespective of the date format in the cells Excel stores dates in a numeric format, e.g. 10/3/97.

3 Centre the field values for the **Order No, Order Date** and **Co. Name** fields. The database should now resemble FIGURE 8.1 above.

4 Double click on the sheet tab. Name the worksheet **ORDERS**.

5 Save the workbook as **DATABASE**.

Task 6: Sorting the database

A common business need is to present the same information in a variety of ways, e.g. in order number sequence (as at present) or in customer name sequence. Sorting involves rearranging the records in a new physical sequence, and speeds up search time once a database gets over a certain length. We can sort the database in order of any field or fields.

Rules and hints for sorting

Sorting will work with any range of worksheet cells, not only databases.

Order of sorting

Field values are sorted in the following order.

■ Numbers.

■ Text.

■ Logical Values.

■ Error Values.

■ Blanks.

You can always undo a sort by selecting **Undo Sort** from the **Edit** menu, provided that you do so immediately.

All the fields in the database, i.e. all columns, must be included in the sort, otherwise any fields omitted from the sort will remain in the same sequence and become attached to the wrong records.

Let's sort the customer orders into date sequence.

1 Select cells A1 to E11 – all fields, all records, including the field names in the header row.

2 Open the **Data** menu and select **Sort**. The **Sort** dialog box appears. If necessary, locate the mouse pointer on the title bar and drag the dialog box down so that the database is visible.

3 Complete the dialog box as follows, using FIGURE 8.4 as a guide.

Sort by At the moment the first field name, **Order No**, is selected.

Click the **down arrow** button on the **Sort By** box. A field list is displayed.

4 Select **Order Date**.

Leave the **Ascending** button on (earliest dates first).

Then by Ignore the next two boxes, we are only sorting by one field.

My list has Leave Header Row selected – the field names in row 1 will not be included in the sort.

The screen should now resemble FIGURE 8.4.

FIGURE 8.4

5 Click the **OK** button.

The ten records are sorted in a new sequence – date order.

 A sort can be changed by either selecting **Undo Sort** from the **Edit** menu, or by another sort operation.

6 **Consolidation – re-sorting records**. Make sure that the cell range A1 to E11 are still selected. Using sections 1 and 2 as a guide, sort the ten records by **Co. Name**.

Notice that strict alphabetical sequence is followed, the record for Patel Industries is placed before Patel Kitchens.

Task 7: Sorting by more than one key

Let's sort the records in reverse date sequence, within **Co. Name.** This means that all the records for, e.g. Wilson Garages, are grouped together, with the latest orders displayed first. This involves two 'keys', **Co. Name** as the primary key and **Order Date** as the secondary key. Make sure that the entire database range is selected as before and issue the **Data-Sort** command.

Complete the **Sort** dialog box as follows, using FIGURE 8.5 as a guide.

1 Ensure that **Co. Name.** is still selected in the first **Sort by:** box.

2 Now click the down arrow box next to the first **Then by:** dialog box.

3 Select **Order Date** from the field list.

4 Click the **Descending** button next to the the first **Then By:** box.

The dialog box should now resemble FIGURE 8.5.

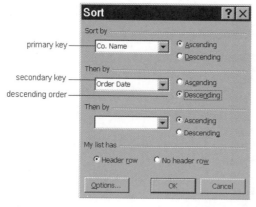

FIGURE 8.5

5 Click the **OK** button.

6 Click on the worksheet to remove the selection highlighting from the database – it should resemble FIGURE 8.6.

	A	B	C	D	E
1	Order No.	Order Date	Co.Ref	Co. Name	Value
2	14008	12-Mar	2245	Goldfield Stables	123.85
3	14009	12-Mar	1289	Marsden Products	1652.54
4	14003	11-Mar	1289	Marsden Products	4456.00
5	14004	10-Mar	2413	Patel Industries	567.00
6	14001	08-Mar	2413	Patel Industries	1466.00
7	14006	10-Mar	2375	Patel Kitchens	55.54
8	14005	11-Mar	955	Tilley Transport	1678.00
9	14002	11-Mar	1453	Wilson Garages	98.76
10	14000	10-Mar	1453	Wilson Garages	3200.00
11	14007	09-Mar	1453	Wilson Garages	2654.00

FIGURE 8.6

7 **Consolidation.** Try sorting the order records as follows

- In descending order of value, i.e. largest orders first.

- By Co. Ref. in ascending date order – compare your result with Appendix 4.

Task 8: Creating new fields by calculation

We are going to add two new fields to the database.

- The **VAT** field will hold the 17.5% VAT to be added to the value of an order.

- The **Total** field which will hold the VAT field added to the order value field.

These new fields will both be calculated by formulae in the usual way.

1 Make sure that the workbook **DATABASE** is open and the worksheet **ORDERS** is the active sheet.

2 Add the two new field names, **VAT** and **Total**, to cells F1 and G1.

3 Centre them in their cells.

4 VAT is 17.5% of Value; move to cell F2 and apply the formula *=E2*0.175*

   Remember to press *Enter*. (* is the multiplication sign)

5 Now copy this formula to the rest of the **VAT** fields using the **Edit-Fill-Down** command.

6 Now calculate the first **Total** field by adding the **VAT** field to the **Value** field. Simply select cell G2 and click the SUM button on the Standard Toolbar (it is marked with a Sigma symbol, like a capital 'M' on its side – Σ).

7 Press *Enter* then **Fill-Down** again.

8 Format the two new fields to two decimal places, using the **Format-Cells-Number** command.

9 Calculated fields can be searched and sorted in the same way as any other fields. To try this, sort the database by the **Total** field (ascending order). Your database should now resemble FIGURE 8.7.

	A	B	C	D	E	F	G
1	Order No.	Order Date	Co.Ref	Co. Name	Value	VAT	Total
2	14006	10-Mar	2375	Patel Kitchens	55.54	9.72	65.26
3	14002	11-Mar	1453	Wilson Garages	98.76	17.28	116.04
4	14008	12-Mar	2245	Goldfield Stables	123.85	21.67	145.52
5	14004	10-Mar	2413	Patel Industries	567.00	99.23	666.23
6	14001	08-Mar	2413	Patel Industries	1466.00	256.55	1722.55
7	14009	12-Mar	1289	Marsden Products	1652.54	289.19	1941.73
8	14005	11-Mar	955	Tilley Transport	1678.00	293.65	1971.65
9	14007	09-Mar	1453	Wilson Garages	2654.00	464.45	3118.45
10	14000	10-Mar	1453	Wilson Garages	3200.00	560.00	3760.00
11	14003	11-Mar	1289	Marsden Products	4456.00	779.80	5235.80
12							

FIGURE 8.7

Task 9: Database maintenance using a Data Form

Obviously all databases need updating as information changes; for example, records will need adding, deleting and amending. You can use a special Excel Data Form to simplify the searching and updating process.

1   Make sure that the **ORDERS** worksheet is the active sheet.

There is no need to select the whole database in order to search or maintain it; simply make sure one of the cells in the database is selected.

2   Select cell D2.

3   Open the Data menu and select the Form option.

A data form is displayed. On the left-hand side of the form are shown the field names and field values for the first record. The form always shows the number of the current record displayed, Number 1 of 10 – see FIGURE 8.8.

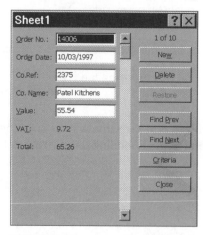

FIGURE 8.8

4   Let's carry out some key database tasks using the command buttons on the right-hand side of the data form.

Find Next button   Click this to scroll forward in the database a record at a time. Notice how, when the field values change, the Record Counter displays the current record – 2 of 10, 3 of 10, etc.

Find Prev. button   Click this to scroll backwards in the database.

Scroll Bar   Moves between records more rapidly. Move to the last record in the database – 10 of 10.

Delete button   Click it once. A message warns you that 'Displayed record will be permanently deleted '. Click the **Cancel** button.

Records deleted with a data form cannot be restored, so make sure that you really want to delete the whole record before going ahead.

Criteria button   Allows you to locate records by named criteria. You will be learning this in more detail in the next section.

Task 10: Some simple searches

Try these two simple searches now.

1   Scroll back to the first record and click the **Criteria** button. A blank record is displayed.

2   Enter your first criterion, *Patel*, in the **Co. Name** field – see FIGURE 8.9.

3   Click the **Find Next** button. The first record matching this search criterion is displayed.

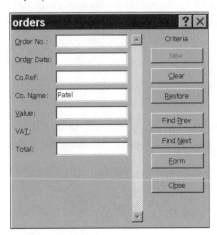

FIGURE 8.9

4 Press the **Find Next** button again to view any further matches.

5　Click the `Find Prev` button to scroll back again. There are three records in all.

Notice that both Patel companies are located – we would need to enter the complete company name to narrow the search further. A 'bleep' informs you when the last matching record is displayed.

6　Press the `Criteria` button again.

Patel is still displayed in the **Co. Name** field.

7　Click the **Value** field and enter the second criterion **<1000**.

8　Click the `Find Next` button. Two records match the combined criteria, i.e. **company name = Patel** and **order value less than £1000**.

9　Click the `Criteria` then the `Clear` buttons to remove the search criteria.

10　Click the `Form` button to return to the data form.

Task 11: Editing data

1　Using the data form, find the record for order number 14005 and amend the Co. Ref to **965**.

The first five data fields can be edited, but the two calculated fields, **VAT** and **Total**, cannot be changed. Their data is produced by formulae which cannot be overwritten. This is why the data in these two fields is not enclosed in boxes – see FIGURE 8.8.

Changes to a record made using a data form are saved *permanently* as soon as you move to another record, even though no specific **Save** command has been given.

The `Restore` button will only undo the change provided you press it before you move to another record.

Press the `Close` button to exit from the data form.

2　**Consolidation**. Using the operations you have just learned, open the data form again and use the `Criteria` button to locate records matching the following conditions.

- Order Total greater than or equal to 3000 (>=)
- Orders placed before 10-Mar (enter the full date 10/03/1997 and use the '<' sign)
- Co. Ref = 1289 and Order No = 14003

Remember to clear the previous search criteria before starting a new search.

Task 12: Adding subtotals to a database

We can total up the values of the orders for each customer using the Subtotal command. This is much quicker and easier than using the SUM function. We can also outline the database and just display the subtotals.

1   Make sure that the **ORDERS** worksheet is the active sheet.

2   Make sure that all the cells in the database are selected, i.e. cell range A1 to G11.

3   Use the *Sort* command to sort the database by Co. Name order – see 'Consolidation – re-sorting records', earlier in this unit.

4   Open the *Data* menu and select *Subtotals*. The whole database is selected and a dialog box opens.

5   Complete the entries as follows, using FIGURE 8.10 as a guide.

At Each Change in   Select the **Co. Name** field from the list box – we want subtotals for each company.

Use Function   Leave this as *SUM,* the default – we want to add the value of orders.

Add Subtotal to   Make sure that **Total** is selected – this is the field value we want to add.

5   Finally click the **OK** button.

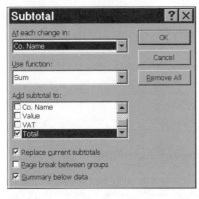

FIGURE 8.10

7   Click the mouse to remove the highlighting. Your database should resemble FIGURE 8.11 below. After each customer a new row is inserted, holding the customer name and the value of their orders subtotalled. At the end of the table a grand total for all orders is displayed – you may need to scroll down to see this.

outline and subtotal buttons

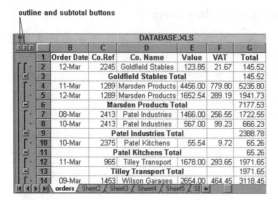

FIGURE 8.11

Task 13: Outlining

At the top left hand corner of the screen are three small buttons, labelled **1**, **2** and **3** – see FIGURE 8.11 above.

1 Click on button **2**. The records are hidden, and only the subtotals and grand total are displayed.

2 Click on button **1**. Only the grand total is displayed.

3 Click on button **3**. The records, subtotals and grand totals are all displayed.

4 Now experiment with the **minus** buttons displayed down the left side of the screen. You will find that you can hide individual groups of records so that only the subtotals are displayed. The button then displays a '**+**' sign. Click the button again and the records are re-displayed.

5 **Removing Subtotals**. Open the Data menu and select Subtotals. The dialog box appears.

6 Click the **Remove All** button. The database is now displayed without subtotals.

Task 14: Searching the database using AutoFilter

The data form that we used in Task 9 has limited search facilities. It can only display one record at a time, and we cannot use 'or' conditions such as ' > 1000 or < 2000' in a data form field. AutoFilter allows you to do this by setting up the search criteria on the worksheet itself. You can then view only those records that you want to view, filtering out or hiding the others.

1 Make sure that the **ORDERS** worksheet is the active sheet.

2 Make sure that one of the cells in the database is selected, i.e. active.

3 Open the **Data** menu and select **Filter**, then the **AutoFilter** option. Arrow boxes appear next to each field name in row 1.

4 Click each arrow in turn. You will see that they contain lists of all the values for that particular field.

5 **Searching by individual field values**. Click the button next to the **Co. Name** field. A list appears.

6 Select **Marsden Products**. Only the records for this company are selected.

7 Click the arrow button on the **Co. Name** field again and select **(all)**. You may have to scroll through the list. All the records are redisplayed.

If you find that you cannot restore all the records then open the **Data** menu and select **Filter**, then the **Show All** option.

8 **Building your own searches**. Let's say that you want to display all records for the 9th or the 11th March. This involves building your own custom search.

Click the **down arrow** on the **Order Date** field and select **(Custom)** from the list. A dialog box appears.

9 Complete the entries as follows, using FIGURE 8.12 as a guide.

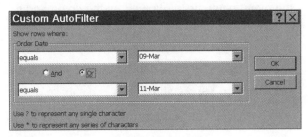

FIGURE 8.12

You have four list boxes to complete plus an **And** or an **Or** button to select.

■ Leave the 'equals' in the top left box as it is.

■ Click the **down arrow** on the top right box and select the date 09-Mar

■ Click the **Or** button.

■ Click the bottom left box and select 'equals'.

■ Click the bottom right arrow box and select the date 11-Mar.

10 Click the **OK** button. The four records that meet the search criteria, 9th March or 11th March, are selected – the rest are hidden – see FIGURE 8.13.

	A	B	C	D	E	F	G
	Order No▼	Order Dat▼	Co.Re▼	Co. Name ▼	Value ▼	VAT ▼	Total ▼
	14003	11-Mar	1289	Marsden Products	4456.00	779.80	5235.80
	14005	11-Mar	965	Tilley Transport	1678.00	293.65	1971.65
	14002	11-Mar	1453	Wilson Garages	98.76	17.28	116.04
	14007	09-Mar	1453	Wilson Garages	2654.00	464.45	3118.45

FIGURE 8.13

11   Click the ▐arrow▐ button on the **Order Date** field heading again. Select (all).
(You may have to scroll through the list.) All the records are redisplayed.

12   **Independent activity**. Use the arrow box on the **Order No.** field to select records
with order numbers between 14005 and 14009.

 You will need to search for numbers >= 14005 and <= 14009.

 Refer to Appendix 5 for guidance on the dialog box entries if necessary.

 Five records should be selected.

13   Open the **Data** menu and select the **Filter-AutoFilter** option. This will de-select
the option and the database will revert to its normal appearance. If you are not
proceding to the next unit then save and close the workbook and exit Excel.

Summary of commands

Menu commands show the menu name first, followed by the command to choose
from the menu, e.g. **Edit-Clear** means open the **Edit** menu and select the **Clear**
command.

Data-Filter-Autofilter	Search database using AutoFilter
Data-Filter-Show All	Show all records in database
Data-Form	Use a data form
Data-Sort	Sort selected cells
Data-Subtotals	Subtotal database/remove subtotals
Edit-Fill-Down	Copy cell values to cells below
Edit-Fill-Series	Create a data series
Edit-Undo Sort	Reverse a sort operation
Format-Cells	Format cells/cell contents
Tool-Options-AutoComplete	Turn AutoComplete on/off

Summary of unit

In this unit you have learned how to

■ plan and build a database

■ insert field names

■ enter data using AutoComplete

■ format fields

■ create a new data series

■ enter order dates

■ sort and re-sort a database

■ sort the database by more than one key

■ create new fields by calculation

■ maintain a database using a Data Form

■ edit data using the Data Form

■ add subtotals to a database

■ search a database using AutoFilter

■ build your own searches.

Linking and copying worksheets

What you will learn in this unit

By the end of this unit you will be able to

- link worksheets together in order to be able to share and exchange data between them
- create a template worksheet
- open and display multiple worksheets
- create a folder
- locate workbooks on disk.

What you should know already

Skill	Covered in
How to start Excel	Unit 1
Basic mouse, Menu and Windows operations	Unit 1
How to create a simple worksheet	Unit 2
How to use simple formulae and formatting	Units 1 – 3

Introduction

This unit shows you how to link worksheets together, so that you can share and exchange data between them. This has a number of advantages.

- You can link several worksheets within one workbook.
- You can edit the linked worksheets as a group; changes made to one worksheet will be reflected in others.
- The Excel windowing facility means that several worksheets can be open in memory at once so that you can see the results of any changes.

A typical linking application is the departments or branches of a company. The same type of financial or numeric data is recorded for each, and they are combined into an overall summary.

Task 1: Creating a template worksheet

We will create two simple worksheets showing the expenses for two departments in a company and then use a third worksheet to summarise them.

We will first create the worksheet framework, copy it and then customise it for each department.

1   Start Excel and open a new workbook.

2   Enter the cell headings and labels shown in FIGURE 9.1.

	A	B	C	D	E	F
1			Expenses - Department			
2						
3			1st Quarter	2nd Quarter	3rd Quarter	4th Quarter
4						
5	Stationery					
6	Telephone					
7	Car Allowance					
8	Public Transport					
9	Salaries					
10						
11	Total					
12						

FIGURE 9.1

3   Double click on the name tab for the worksheet – it should be highlighted.

4 Change the sheet name to **Department A**.

Task 2: Copying cells between worksheets

1   Now select the cell range A1 to F11.

2   Open the **Edit** menu and select **Copy**.

3   Click the sheet tab for **Sheet2** .

4   Select cell A1 in Sheet2.

5   Open the **Edit** menu and select **Paste**.

The cells are copied into Sheet2.

6   Change the sheet name for Sheet2 to **Department B**.

7   Repeat the above operations to create a third sheet containing the same data. Name it **SUMMARY 1**.

8   Now we need to enter the individual expenses for departments A and B. Amend the sheet Department A as shown in FIGURE 9.2. Create the totals in row 11 using formulae.

	A	B	C	D	E	F
1			Expenses - Department A			
2						
3			1st Quarter	2nd Quarter	3rd Quarter	4th Quarter
4						
5	Stationery		452	387	299	354
6	Telephone		658	591	710	589
7	Car Allowance		436	587	687	499
8	Public Transport		65	43	58	39
9	Salaries		10345	9835	10583	10976
10						
11	Total		11956	11443	12337	12457
12						

FIGURE 9.2

9   Similarly amend the sheet **Department B** as shown in FIGURE 9.3. Create the totals in row 11 using formulae as before.

	A	B	C	D	E	F
1			Expenses - Department B			
2						
3			1st Quarter	2nd Quarter	3rd Quarter	4th Quarter
4						
5	Stationery		593	481	428	519
6	Telephone		765	698	731	624
7	Car Allowance		616	790	687	502
8	Public Transport		76	67	89	53
9	Salaries		18371	16318	17034	14978
10						
11	Total		20421	18354	18969	16676

FIGURE 9.3

Task 3: Opening and displaying multiple worksheets

We will use the **SUMMARY 1** worksheet to combine the two sets of departmental totals. First we need to display the three sheets in separate windows.

There are several ways of arranging the three worksheet windows on screen using the **Window-Arrange** menu.

1   Make sure that **Department A** is the active sheet.

2   Open the **Window** menu and select **New Window**. A second window appears, overlaying the first.

3   Click the **Department B sheet** tab in this window.

4   Open the **Window** menu and select **New Window** again.

5   Click the **Summary 1** tab in this window. We now have three worksheets open in their own windows.

Task 4 Arranging multiple worksheets

1 Open the Window menu and select the Arrange option. A dialog box appears.

2 Click the Cascade option, then OK

You should now be able to see the overlapping edges of the 3 worksheets – see FIGURE 9.4. If you can only see one worksheet then you probably need to use the Restore button to reduce the window size.

edges of the 3
worksheets in
tiled display

FIGURE 9.4

3 To practise moving between worksheet windows do either of the following:

■ Click on the edge of a worksheet (left or right side), or

■ Use the Window menu to select a worksheet – this is useful if you cannot see the worksheet. However the menu refers to them by number, e.g. **BOOK1:1**, rather than by name.

After a while the arrangement may become jumbled and worksheets become hidden, if so open the Window menu and take the **Arrange-Cascade** options again. If a workbook appears blank, check that the correct sheet is active and that the correct cells are displayed (press the *Ctrl* and *Home* keys together to go to the top of the worksheet).

4 Open the Window menu and take the Arrange option again.

5 This time click the Tiled option then OK.

The workbooks are arranged side by side on the screen – see FIGURE 9.5.

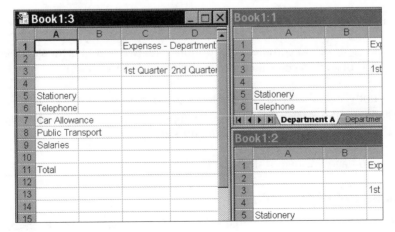

FIGURE 9.5

6   It doesn't matter if your workbooks are in a different order to that shown in FIGURE 9.5. Click on each workbook in turn – it becomes the active workbook (the Title Bar is blue).

Task 5: Linking worksheets

We can now use the worksheet **SUMMARY 1** to link the two other worksheets using external references. We want to create a formula that adds together the contents of, for example, cell C5 for the two departments and places them in cell C5 in the summary worksheet.

1   Click cell C5 in the **SUMMARY 1** worksheet. This activates both the worksheet and the cell.

2   To begin a formula type *=SUM(* in the cell.

Rather than type a complex formula it is easier first to click the worksheet to activate it, then the cell to be included in the formula.

3   Click the worksheet **Department A** to activate it.

4   Click cell C5 in this worksheet.

5   Now check the Formula Bar.

It should read **=SUM('Department A'!C5**

6   Click the Formula Bar and type a **+** sign on the end of this formula.

7   Click the worksheet **Department B** to activate it.

8   Click cell C5 in this worksheet.

9   Now check the Formula Bar.

It should read: =SUM('Department A'!C5 +'Department B'!C5

10   Press the *Enter* key to complete the formula. The two amounts for stationery are added and placed in cell C5 of the summary worksheet (1045).

If a cell is not visible then you can use the scroll bars to scroll it into view. Alternatively use the Maximize button to temporarily enlarge the workbook. If you have made a mistake, delete the formula and start again.

11   When you have finished, restore the tiled view.

Explanation of the formula

This linking formula contains external references to two worksheets. Each external reference must consist of the full sheet name plus the cell reference, both separated by an exclamation mark. An error message indicates that the formula is wrongly typed. If the formula is correct then Excel will add the final bracket to the formula.

Task 6 Copying linking formulae

1   Maximise the **SUMMARY 1** workbook.

2   Select cells C5 to F5. Then use **Edit-Fill-Right**. The linking formulae, with their external references, are copied to the other cells.

3   Now select the cell range C5 to F11. Select the **Edit-Fill-Down** options.

4   Next select cell range C10 to F10. Press the *Delete* key to clear their contents.

The **SUMMARY 1** workbook should now resemble FIGURE 9.6 – check the totals.

	A	B	C	D	E	F
1			Summary of Expenses - Departments A & B			
2						
3			1st Quarter	2nd Quarter	3rd Quarter	4th Quarter
4						
5	Stationery		1045	868	727	873
6	Telephone		1423	1289	1441	1213
7	Car Allowance		1052	1377	1374	1001
8	Public Transport		141	110	147	92
9	Salaries		28716	26153	27617	25954
10						
11	Total		32377	29797	31306	29133
12						

FIGURE 9.6

5   Use the **Window-Arrange** command to view the three workbooks in tiled display again if necessary. Changes made to any of the supporting worksheets – **Department A** or **Department B** – will be reflected in the summary or dependent workbook – **SUMMARY 1**.

6   Try the following 'what if' experiment. At the moment the total expenses for the first quarter are £32,377 – see cell C11 in the worksheet **SUMMARY 1**. The target is £30,000.

7   Amend the salaries amount for the first quarter for the **Department A** and **Department B** worksheets to 8500 and 17000 respectively.

8   Now activate the **SUMMARY 1** workbook and look at cell C11 – the target is now achieved. The summary total is now £29,161.

9   Undo these changes using the **Edit** menu to see their effect again.

10   At the moment each worksheet is open in its own window; close two of these windows using the **Close** button at the top right of the worksheet windows.

11 Maximise the remaining worksheet window. You can now use the sheet tabs to move between the three worksheets in the usual way.

Task 7: Creating a folder

We will save the workbook and create a folder in which to store it.

These instructions assume that you are saving your work to diskette, if not then substitute the appropriate drive.

1 Open the **File** menu and select **Save as**.

A dialog box appears. Use FIGURE 9.7 as a guide to completing it.

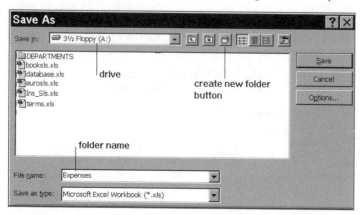

FIGURE 9.7

2 Move the mouse pointer onto the **Create New Folder** button. An identifying screen tip box will open.

3 Click the button. A dialog box appears.

4 Name the new folder **DEPARTMENTS**. Click **OK** The folder appears in the list of workbook files.

5 Select the **File Name** box. Enter the name *EXPENSES*.

6 Click the down arrow on the **Save in:** box.

7 Select the drive **3½ Floppy(A:)**.

8 Double click on the folder icon **DEPARTMENTS**. It now appears in the **Save in:** box.

9 Click the **Save** button.

The workbook **EXPENSES** is saved in the **DEPARTMENTS** folder.

Task 8: Locating workbooks on disk

In the previous task we saved a worksheet in a folder. If you save without specifying the folder or the drive then a file will be saved in whichever drive and folder happen to be in use at the time. Often this is the Excel folder itself and you end up saving your data files (workbooks) in the same folder as Excel *program* files. This is not a good idea for several reasons.

- They are hard to find in a long list of other files.

- If you erase the Excel files when you are updating to a new release of Excel then your data files will get deleted too.

- You may well end up with files scattered over various disks and drives.

Folders are a useful unit of organisation; however it is easy to forget which folder the files are stored in. The folder structure can also get quite complex with many levels of files and subfolders within other folders. Fortunately Excel provides a powerful search facility to locate files.

 These instructions assume that you have created the workbooks mentioned in previous units and are saving your work to diskette; if not then substitute an appropriate drive or workbook.

1 Make sure that Excel is running but close any open workbooks. If you have been saving your workbooks to diskette then make sure it is in the diskette drive.

2 Open the **File** menu and select **Open.**

The **Open** dialog box is displayed – see FIGURE 9.8.

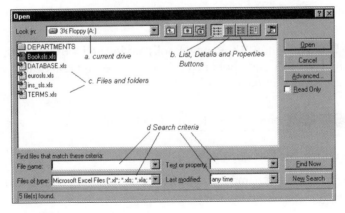

FIGURE 9.8

 The current drive and/or folder is shown in the **Look in** box. Change it to **3½ Floppy** (**A:**) if necessary. Various buttons are displayed on the right of the dialog box.

The folders and/or workbook files on the current drive are displayed.

The search criteria are displayed at the bottom of the dialog box. You can search by name, contents, file type and date.

133

4 **More details on a file.** First click the `List` button.

5 Select any file from the list.

6 Click the `Details` button. Full file details are given – its size, type and date of creation or last modification.

7 Try this for a few other files.

8 **File properties.** Click the `Properties` button. The name of the file's creator is also given.

9 Click the `List` button.

10 **Opening a folder.** Double click the **DEPARTMENTS** folder. It opens becoming the current folder. The workbook **EXPENSES** that you created in the last activity is shown.

11 Click the down arrow on the **Look in** box and re-select the drive again, e.g. **3¹/₂ Floppy (A:)**.The **DEPARTMENTS** folder is closed and the files on the main drive are re-displayed.

Task 9: Searching for a file by name

Let's locate all the files with the letters 'sls' in their name.

1 Enter *sls* in the **File Name** box.

2 Click the `Find Now` button. Three workbooks are located – **BOOKSLS, EUROSLS** and **INS_SLS** and could be opened if so desired (this search will only work if they are located in the current folder).

3 Click the `New search` button to re-display the other files.

Task 10: Searching by file contents

If you can't remember the file name then you can search for files by their contents, e.g. ones that contain data about holidays.

1 Enter the word *holiday* in the **Text or property** box.

2 Click the `Find now` button.

One workbook is located – **EUROSLS**, plus any folders.

3 Click the `New search` button to re-display the other files.

4   If you are not proceding to the next unit then cancel the Open dialog box and exit Excel.

Summary of commands

Menu commands show the menu name first, followed by the command to choose from the menu, e.g. **Edit-Clear** means open the **Edit** menu and select the **Clear** command.

Edit-Copy	Copy selected cell(s)
Edit-Paste	Insert cut or copied cells
Edit-Fill-Right	Copy selected cells to selected right hand columns
Edit-Fill-Down	Copy selected cells into selected lower rows
File-Close	Close current workbook
File-Open	Open an existing workbook
File-Save as	Save a new workbook, or copy an existing workbook under a new name
Window-Arrange	Arrange open windows
Window-New Window	Display workbook or worksheet in own window

Summary of unit

In this unit you have learned how to

- create a template worksheet
- copy cells between worksheets
- open and display multiple worksheets
- arrange multiple worksheets
- link worksheets
- copy linking formulae
- create a folder
- locate workbooks on disk
- search for files by name and by file contents.

unit 10

Copying and linking workbooks

What you will learn in this unit

By the time you have completed this unit you will be able to

- copy and link workbooks
- maintain links between workbooks.

What you should know already

Skill	Covered in
How to start Excel	Unit 1
Basic mouse, menu and Windows operations	Unit 1
How to create a simple worksheet	Unit 2
How to use simple formulae and formatting	Units 1 – 3

What you will need

To complete this unti you will need

- the workbook **EXPENSES**, created in the previous unit in the folder **DEPARTMENTS**.

Introduction

Unit 9 showed you how to link worksheets within a workbook. This unit shows you how to link separate workbooks together. There are cases where separate linked workbooks are better than linked worksheets. For example, it may be more convenient for several workbooks to be created independently and combined and summarised later.

Task 1: Copying a workbook under a new name

1 Open the **EXPENSES** workbook. It is in the **DEPARTMENTS** folder – see previous unit if necessary.

2 Open the File menu and select Save As (not Save).

A dialog box appears – see FIGURE 10.1 for guidance.

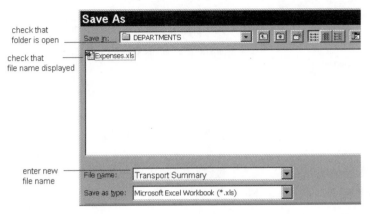

FIGURE 10.1

3   The **File Name** box contains the current name **EXPENSES**.

4   Enter the new name *TRANSPORT SUMMARY*.

5   Check that the folder name **DEPARTMENTS** appears in the **Save in** box.

6   Click the **Save** button. The original workbook **EXPENSES** is copied under the new name **TRANSPORT SUMMARY** and then closed, leaving the **TRANSPORT SUMMARY** workbook displayed.

7   Use the **Edit-Delete Sheet** command to delete the worksheets **DEPARTMENT A** and **DEPARTMENT B** from the **TRANSPORT SUMMARY** workbook. The **SUMMARY 1** worksheet will now display a number of errors, as it contains external formulae based on these two deleted worksheets.

8   Now select rows 4 to 6 and use the **Edit-Delete** command to remove them.

9   Similarly delete the new row 6 containing the salaries data.

10   Delete the contents of cell range C4 to F7.

11   Rename the **SUMMARY 1** worksheet **SUMMARY 2** and amend the title in row 1. The worksheet should now look like FIGURE 10.2.

	A	B	C	D	E	F
1			Summary of Transport Expenses - Departments A & I			
2						
3			1st Quarter	2nd Quarter	3rd Quarter	4th Quarter
4	Car Allowance					
5	Public Transport					
6						
7	Total					
8						
9						
10						
11						
12						

⏮ ◀ ▶ ⏭ Summary 2

FIGURE 10.2

Task 2: Handling multiple workbooks

Open the two workbooks – **EXPENSES** and **TRANSPORT SUMMARY**. There are several ways of arranging the workbook windows on screen using the **Window-Arrange** menu – see Unit 9, Task 3.

1   Open the **Window** menu and take the **Arrange** option.

2   Click the **Tiled** option, then **OK**   The two workbooks are arranged side by side on the screen – see FIGURE 10.3.

🖼 transport summary.xls	_ □ ✕	Expenses.xls		
B	C	D	A	B
2			1		Sun
3	1st Quarter	2nd Quarter	3rd Q	2	
4			3		1st
5			4		
6			5 Stationery	
7			6 Telephone	
8			7 Car Allowance	
9			8 Public Transport	
10			9 Salaries	
11			10	

⏮ ◀ ▶ ⏭ Summary 2   ◀   ▶   ⏮ ◀ ▶ ⏭ Department A / Department E

FIGURE 10.3

It doesn't matter if your workbooks are in a different order to that shown in FIGURE 10.3.

3   Click on each workbook in turn – it becomes the active workbook (the Title Bar is blue).

Task 3: Linking workbooks with formulae

1   Now select the **TRANSPORT SUMMARY** workbook.

2   Select cell C4 of the **SUMMARY 2** worksheet.

3 Enter an = sign to start a formula.

4 Click the **EXPENSES** workbook.

5 Click cell C7 in the **SUMMARY 1** worksheet.

The cell is enclosed in a dotted rectangle and the following linking formula appears in cell C4 of the **SUMMARY 2** worksheet:
='[Expenses.xls]Summary 1'!$C$7
Compare your workbook with FIGURE 10.4 if necessary.

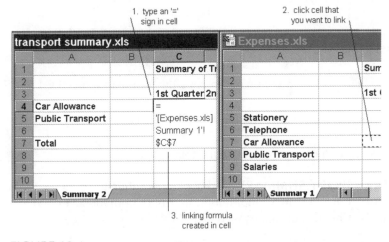

FIGURE 10.4

6 Press the _Enter_ key and it appears in the Formula Bar of the **TRANSPORT SUMMARY** workbook.

 If rows 4 and 7 are not visible then you can use the scroll bars to scroll them into view. Alternatively use the Maximize button to temporarily enlarge the workbook.

7 When you have finished click the Restore button to restore the tiled view – see FIGURE 10.3.

Explanation of the linking formula

In order to link workbooks you need an external reference. Each external reference must consist of the full name of the external workbook in square brackets, plus the worksheet name – both are enclosed in single quotes e.g. '[Expenses.xls]Summary 1'. They are separated from the cell references by an exclamation mark, e.g. !$C$7.

 The dollar signs in the formula make it into an _absolute_ reference. This means that when we copy the formula into another cell, the cell address C7 will not be adjusted to reflect its new location. Sometimes this is useful – see unit 4, Task 7, 'Explanation of the formula'. where absolute and relative references are explained – but in this case we need it to be a _relative_ reference. This means that the cell reference in formulae will be automatically adjusted when cells are copied.

8   Select cell C4 if necessary then select the Formula Bar.

9   Remove the two dollar signs from the formula.

It should now read: **='[Expenses.xls]Summary 1'!C7**

10   Press the *Enter* key.

11   Maximise the **TRANSPORT SUMMARY** workbook.

12   Select the cell range C4 to F4.

13   Open the **Edit** menu and select the **Fill-Right** command. The linking formula is copied to the whole cell range.

14   Use the **Edit-Fill-Down** command to copy the formula from cell C4 to C5   .

15   Repeat the **Fill-Right** operation for the cell range C5 to F5.

16   Use the **SUM** function to calculate the totals in row 7.

The **TRANSPORT SUMMARY** workbook now summarises the two transport categories 'Car Allowance' and 'Public Transport' from the **EXPENSES** workbook. Check your figures with FIGURE 10.5.

	A	B	C	D	E	F
1			Summary of Transport Expenses - Departments A & E			
2						
3			1st Quarter	2nd Quarter	3rd Quarter	4th Quarter
4	Car Allowance		1052	1377	1374	1001
5	Public Transport		141	110	147	92
6						
7	Total		1193	1487	1521	1093
8						

FIGURE 10.5

17   Use the **Window-Arrange** command to view the two workbooks in tiled display again if necessary. Changes made to the supporting worksheet – **Expenses** – will be reflected in the summary or dependent workbook **TRANSPORT SUMMARY**.

18   Try the following experiment. Select the **EXPENSES** workbook and select the worksheet **Department A.**

19   Amend cell C8 to **100** and press *Enter*.

The value of the dependent cell C5 in the Summary 2 sheet of the workbook **TRANSPORT SUMMARY** also changes – to 176.

20   Use the **Edit-Undo** command to reverse the change.

21   Save and close both workbooks and exit from Excel.

Task 4: Maintaining links between workbooks

Excel 'remembers' the links between workbooks, even if the workbooks are opened and closed at different times. You will be prompted to update the links.

1   Start Excel again and open the **TRANSPORT SUMMARY** workbook (the dependent workbook). A dialog box appears, prompting you to update the links with any changes made to the other workbook (the supporting workbook).

2   Click the **Yes** button.

3   Open the **EXPENSES** workbook. You are not prompted to save any links in this case as **EXPENSES** is the supporting workbook and not affected by any changes to the dependent workbook **TRANSPORT SUMMARY**.

Task 5: Adding comments to a workbook

1   Make **TRANSPORT SUMMARY** the active workbook.

2   Open the File menu and select Properties.

3   Make sure that the **Summary** tab is selected.

4   The Summary dialog box allows you to add a title, subject and brief summary of the workbook. Do this.

 If you select Save preview picture at the bottom of the dialog box then you will be able to preview the workbook before opening it using the Open dialog box. This facility is useful for large files that take a long time to load.

5   Close the two workbooks.

Summary of commands

Menu commands show the menu name first, followed by the command to choose from the menu, e.g. Edit-Clear means open the **Edit** menu and select the Clear command.

Edit-Delete	Delete selected worksheet element(s)
Edit-Delete Sheet	Delete selected worksheet
Edit-Fill-Right/Down	Copy selected cells to selected right hand/ lower columns
File-Properties-Summary	Add comment to a workbook
File-Open	Open an existing workbook
File-Save as	Save a new workbook, or copy an existing workbook under a new name
Window-Arrange	Arrange windows on screen

Summary of unit

In this unit you have learned how to

- copy a workbook under a new name
- handle multiple workbooks
- link workbooks using formulae
- maintain links between workbooks
- add comments to a workbook.

Excel analysis tools – Goal Seek and Solver

What you will learn in this unit

By the end of this unit you will be able to

- use Goal Seek to change variables in order to achieve target values
- use Solver to manipulate values in order to produce optimum targets.

What you should know already

Skill	Covered in
How to start Excel	Unit 1
Basic mouse, menu and Windows operations	Unit 1
How to create a simple worksheet	Unit 1
How to use simple formulae and formatting	Units 1 – 3

Introduction

In the next few tasks we will look at the special-purpose analysis tools Goal Seek and Solver. These two tools also automate the process of repeated 'What if?' trials.

Task 1: Goal Seek

The 'What-if?' abilities of Excel allow us to try out alternative values for a given situation. The first and simplest is Goal Seek. Often you want to know what value a variable needs to be for a formula to equal a particular value. Goal Seek keeps changing the value of the variable until the formula achieves the target value.

1   Open a new workbook and create the simple worksheet shown in FIGURE 11.1.

 First open the **Tools** menu and check that **Goal Seek** and **Solver** are listed as options. If not then select the **Add-Ins** option on the Tools menu. (You need to open a new workbook to do this – see Task 1 below.) If they are listed then you can open them now. If not then they will need to be installed, using a set of Excel or Office 97 disks or CD-ROM.

2   Use formulae to create the totals in column D and row 8.

3   Format all the numbers to whole numbers.

4   Save the workbook as **PROFITS**.

	A	B	C	D	E
1					
2		No of	Profit	Profit	
3		Units	pre Unit		
4					
5	Product A	100	46	4600	
6	Product B	100	53	5300	
7	Product C	100	69	6900	
8	Totals	300		16800	
9					
10					
11					

FIGURE 11.1

5   Open the **Tools** menu and select **Goal Seek**. A dialog box appears.

6   If necessary, move the box so that you can see column C – see FIGURE 11.2. You need to position the screen pointer on the title of the box, and drag it using the mouse. Alternatively you can use the **Collapse** button, located next to the data entry boxes on the dialog box, to reduce its size.

	A	B	C	D	E	F	G	H
1								
2		No of	Profit	Profit		**Goal Seek**		? ✕
3		Units	pre Unit					
4						Set cell:	D8	
5	Product A	100	46	4600		To value:	20000	
6	Product B	100	53	5300		By changing cell:	B6	
7	Product C	100	69	6900				
8	Totals	300		16800		OK	Cancel	
9								
10								
11								

FIGURE 11.2

7   We want to find out how many of product B we need to make to raise total profits from £16,800 to £20,000.

Complete the box as shown in FIGURE 11.2 above, i.e.

Set cell   D8

To value   20000

By changing cell B6.

8   Make a note of the present value of cell B6. Click **OK**.

A further **Goal seek Status** dialog box appears reporting the solution. The value of cell B6 is changed to 160 – the number of product B needed to reach the £20,000 goal.

9   Click the **Cancel** button. This restores the previous value for cell B6 and all the dependent cells. If you click **OK** by accident then select **Undo** from the **Edit** menu.

10 Now try the following Goal Seek: What profit per unit for Product C (cell C7) would achieve a total profit of £18,000?

Consolidation

■ Open the workbook **TERMS.XLS** created in Unit 2.

■ Make **Spring Term** the active sheet.

■ Scroll to week 9. How large a bank loan would you need in week 9 to achieve a closing balance of £150 in week 9?

Notes on Goal Seek

The **Goal Seek Status** dialog box displays two extra buttons.

■ **Pause** – allows you to pause during goal seeking.

■ **Step** – allows you to continue one step at a time.

 Goal seeking will only work if the cell whose value you set contains a value, not a formula. The cell whose value you set must be related by a formula to the cell whose target value you are changing.

Task 2: Solver

Goal Seek used in the previous task can substitute various values for a variable in a formula but cannot determine what are the 'best' ones for your purpose. Solver, as its name suggests, can solve certain types of problem. It will juggle with multiple values for variables and find the combination producing the optimum or target result, e.g. it can determine the most profitable mix of products, schedule staff to minimise the wages bill, or allocate working capital to its most profitable use. Solver allows you to specify up to two hundred variables; it also allows you to put constraints on variables by specifying the limits that they can take, e.g. minimum and maximum values for a machine's output or for a working week.

However, to use Solver effectively you must thoroughly understand the nature of the problem that you are trying to solve, otherwise Solver will either fail to work altogether or give you misleading results. For complex problems there may well be more than one solution and you may need to run Solver more than once with different ranges of values.

Make sure that the workbook **PROFITS** that you used in Task 1 is still open.

We wish to make a profit of £20,000 for the three products subject to the following four constraints, which are based on production capacity and customer demand.

i) The maximum number we can make of Product A (cell B5) is 50.

ii and iii) We must make at least 40 each of Products B and C (cells B6 and B7).

iv) Overall production can rise to a maximum of 350 (cell B8).

We need to enter these constraints into Solver and run it.

1 Open the **Tools** menu and select **Solver.** If Solver does not start then it will need to be installed, using a set of Excel 97 or Office 97 disks or CD-ROM.

The **Solver Parameters** dialog box appears – FIGURE 11.3 shows the completed parameters.

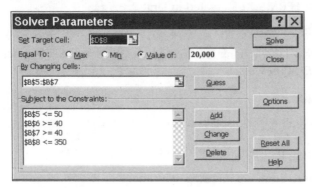

FIGURE 11.3

2 Complete the first part of the dialog box as follows, using FIGURE 11.3 as a guide.

(You can either type in the cell references or click on the appropriate cells in the worksheet. Solver converts the cell references to absolute references after you enter them.)

Set Target Cell:	Enter D8
Equal to buttons:	Make sure that **Value of** is selected and that 20,000 is entered

3 Click the **By Changing Cells** box and enter *B5:B7*. We want to vary the cells containing the number of units made for each product.

4 We must apply the first constraint now – the maximum number we can make of Product A is 50. Click the **Add** button. A new dialog box appears **Add Constraint**.

5 Add the following constraint using FIGURE 11.4 below as a guide.

6 Insert the cell references B5 in the **Cell reference** box.

7 Select the relationship <= in the middle box.

8 Click the **Constraint** box and insert *50*.

9 Click **OK** .

You are returned to the **Solver Parameters** dialog box. The constraint is shown –

$B$5<=50. (Solver converts the cell references to absolute references.) If you
have made an error then click either the **Change** button to edit it, or the
Delete button and start again.

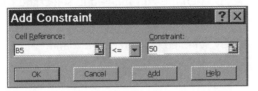

FIGURE 11.4

10 Add the second two constraints in the same way – we must make at least 40
each of Products B and C.

The constraints are **B6 >= 40** and **B7>=40** – make sure that you use the '>' sign.

11 Add the fourth and final constraint – see FIGURE 11.3 above.

You have now finished your Solver parameters.

Cancel the **Add Constraint** box if necessary.

12 Click the **Solve** button. Solver goes through a complex series of calculations
until it reaches the first valid solution. The worksheet values are modified to
show it. A **Solver results** dialog box appears; move this aside so that you can see
the solution – all four constraints have been met – see FIGURE 11.5.

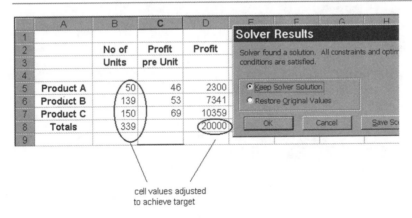

cell values adjusted
to achieve target

FIGURE 11.5

The **Solver Results** dialog box offers you the option of keeping the Solver
solution or restoring the original values.

13 Click the **Restore Original Values** button, then click **OK**.

14 Save and close the workbook.

Summary of commands

Menu commands show the menu name first, followed by the command to choose from the menu, e.g. **Edit-Clear** means open the **Edit** menu and select the **Clear** command.

Edit-Fill-Right	Copy selected cells into right-hand columns
Format-Cells-Number	Format numeric values
Insert-Name-Define	Create a name, e.g. for a cell
Tools-Goal Seek	Change values of selected cell(s) so formula achieves a specified target value
Tools-Add-Ins	Install Goal Seek or Solver
Tools-Solver	Use Solver

Summary of unit

In this unit you have learned how to

- change values using Goal Seek to achieve target values

- use Solver to solve problems involving combinations of multiple values to produce optimum results.

Excel Functions

What you will learn in this unit

By the end of this unit you will be able to

■ use some of the simpler Excel functions, including table functions

What you should know already

Skill	Covered in
How to start Excel	Unit 1
Basic mouse, menu and Windows operations	Unit 1
How to create a simple worksheet	Unit 2
How to use simple formulae and formatting	Units 2 – 3

What you need

To complete this unit you will need

■ **BOOKSLS** created in Unit 7.

Introduction

It is beyond the scope of these units to deal with all of the Excel functions; many, such as trigonometric and engineering functions, have little general business application. To use others, such as financial functions, you need some specialist background in the subject to understand the significance of the results. Some functions we have already used, such as the simpler maths functions. In the first section of this unit, we review the various types of functions; in Task 3 we will use a lookup function. In Tasks 4 to 8 we use some other widely used functions. Other useful functions are listed at the end of this unit.

Notes on using functions

■ Functions are ready-made formulae that perform useful calculations.

■ They produce their result in the cell in which they are entered.

■ Every function must start with the = sign.

■ Functions can be entered in lower or upper case. It is a good idea to type functions in lower case – if Excel converts it to upper case then you know that it is typed correctly.

■ Normally a function contains no spaces.

149

- Functions can form part of a formula – or another function.

- Functions require you to supply information for their operations, called arguments, e.g. SUM(range) requires the cell range argument to be added.

- Arguments are enclosed in round brackets – () these *must* be typed. Optional arguments are shown in the lists that follow in square brackets – [ ]. These brackets are for your guidance only and should *not* be typed.

- Two or more arguments are separated by commas. The commas *must* be typed if more than one argument is used.

- You can either type the function yourself or use Paste Function, which lets you choose the function from a list and paste it into a cell.

Task 1: Types of functions

1   Open a new workbook.

2   Open the **Insert** menu and select the **Function** option (or use the
    Paste Function button on the Standard Toolbar marked 'fx').

    The **Paste Function** dialog box appears, listing 11 categories of functions – see
    FIGURE 12.1. If the **Office Assistant** dialog box opens then read the note to Task
    2 below – you may decide to use it as supplementary guidance in this activity.

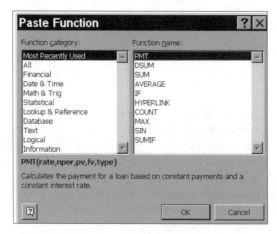

FIGURE 12.1

3   Click the first Function Category – **Most Recently Used**. In the right-hand box –
    Function Name – are some of the functions we have used so far.

4   Click each function in turn. The syntax of the function and a brief explanation
    are given at the bottom of the dialog box.

5   Click the second function category – **All**. All the functions are listed
    alphabetically in the **Function Name** box.

Now carry on reviewing the other Function Categories listed below in the same way.

Financial Functions are used to calculate depreciation, return on investments etc. Two of these functions are used in Task 8.

Date and Time Functions are used in Tasks 4 and 7.

Mathematical and Trigonometric Functions calculate square roots, cosines etc. as well as the simpler functions such as *SUM*.

Statistical Functions such as average and standard deviation are used in Task 5.

Lookup and Reference Functions are used to look up values in cells and tables. We will use one in Task 3.

Database Functions carry out operations on database records only, e.g. summing or averaging selected records.

Text Functions manipulate strings of text, e.g. finding the length or converting to upper case. Two examples are given under Text functions, at the end of this unit.

Logical Functions test for the truth of certain conditions. An *IF* condition is used in Task 6.

Information Functions test and report on cell references and contents, e.g. blanks or errors. Two examples are given at the end of this unit under 'Information functions'.

Task 2   Help on Functions – using the Office Assistant

When you start Paste Function the **Office Assistant** dialog box may be displayed too. If not click the **Office Assistant** button (marked with a '?') in the bottom left-hand corner of the **Paste Function** dialog box. If nothing happens then Office Assistant has not been installed, in which case continue with Task 3.

1 Click the **Financial Function** Category, then select **FV**. (This stands for Future Value)

2 Click the **Office Assistant** (animated paperclip) logo.

3 Take the **'Help with this feature'** option in the Office Assistant. A further dialog box appears.

4 Click the **Help on selected function** button. Help text explaining the Future Value function is displayed.

5 Close the Help window. You are returned to the **Paste Function** dialog box.

6 Close the Office Assistant window.

Note

At stage 3 above it is also possible to enter a brief description e.g. *'find the minimum value in a database'* and click the **Search** button. Office Assistant should select one or two functions for you to choose, including the appropriate one *DMIN*. Successful searches depend on your skill in finding the appropriate search terms; you can keep trying until you narrow down the search results to the ones that you want. For example, try substituting the word 'lowest' for 'minimum' in your description and Office Assistant doesn't perform as well. You can also just type in keywords rather than a complete sentence, e.g. *'database'* and *'minimum'*.

7 Click the **Cancel** button on the **Paste Function** dialog box. You are returned to the blank worksheet.

Task 3: Lookup tables

Lookup tables can be used to hold various types of fixed information that can be 'looked up' from another part of the worksheet, e.g. rates of pay, credit ratings or addresses. We will use a *LOOKUP* function to do this. Look at FIGURE 12.2 below.

	A	B	C	D	E	F	G
1				Order Discount Look-up			
2							
3	Cash Order						
4	Order Value:						
5	Discount						
6	Net Value			Order Value	Cash	Credit	
7				0	5%	0%	
8	Credit Order			500	10%	5%	
9	Order Value:			1000	15%	10%	
10	Discount			5000	20%	15%	
11	Net Value			10000	25%	20%	
12							

FIGURE 12.2

In columns D to F is a table to look up customer discounts, based on the order value – from £0 to £10,000 – and the type of order (cash or credit). As the discount rates in the table do not follow any obvious numeric sequence, using a formula to generate them would be difficult.

You can use two lookup functions to get data from a table, *HLOOKUP* and *VLOOKUP: HLOOKUP* is used if the lookup values are arranged horizontally in a row.

The syntax is *=HLOOKUP(x,range,index)*

VLOOKUP is used if the lookup values are arranged vertically in a column, as they are in the table shown above (the more usual arrangement). The syntax is *=VLOOKUP(x,range,index)*

x is the value that you want to look up; it can be entered as text, a number or a cell reference.

Range is the range of cells forming the table.

Index tells you which column or row to look in.

Applying this to FIGURE 12.2 above:

x is cell B4 where the value of the cash order will be entered,

Range is the cell range D7 to F11 holding the lookup table,

Index are columns E and F where the the lookup values are held.

 For the **LOOKUP** function to work, the first column of the lookup table must consist of entries that are used to look up items of data in immediately adjacent columns. These entries must be unique and in ascending order.

1 Open a new workbook.

2 Create the data as shown in FIGURE 12.2 above and enter an order value of 600 in cell B4.

3 In cell B5 enter the formula *=vlookup(b4,d7:f11,2)*

Enter it in lower case – if it is correct, it is converted to upper case.

The formula means 'look up the value in cell B4, from the table in cell range D7 to F11, in the 2nd column of the table'.

The lookup function searches the first column of compare values – column D – until it reaches a number equal to or higher than 600 (cell D9) It then goes back a row if it is higher (to cell D8), then goes to the second column (E) and looks up the discount of 10% (in cell E8). For this reason the values in the first column of the lookup table – column D – must be in ascending sequence. The discount is displayed as 0.1.

4 Use the **Format-Cells** command. Select the **Number** tab.

5 From the dialog box select **Percentage** from the category list.

6 Select 0 from decimal places box and click **OK**. The discount is now displayed as 10% in cell B5. The formula to calculate the net value of the order (i.e. order value minus discount) can now be entered in cell B6.

7 Enter the formula *= B4-(B4*B5)* in this cell. The order value minus discount is shown in cell B6 – the value should be 540.

8 Try entering some other order values in cell B4 to test this.

9 **Consolidation**. Now repeat these steps and enter another ***VLOOKUP*** formula in cell B10 to calculate the discount on credit orders.

 You will need to modify the cell references, i.e. the cell reference for the   lookup value (B9) and the column number (3) where the lookup values are held.

10 Enter a credit order value of ***10,000*** in cell B9.

11 Check that the discount is 20% and the net order value is 8,000.

12 Save the workbook as **DISCOUNT** and close it.

Using Excel functions

In the first section of this unit we reviewed the major categories of function. We shall try some of them out now, bearing in mind that these only represent a fraction of those available.

Look at the worksheet in FIGURE 12.3; it monitors the performance of the shares of a travel company over a two week period (weekends excluded). Open a new workbook. By now you should be able to enter the initial worksheet for yourself. Here, we shall concentrate on the functions.

	A	B	C
1		Share Analysis	
2			
3	Date	Alpha	
4		Tours	
5	1-Sep	19.44	
6	2-Sep	19.44	
7	3-Sep	20.65	
8	4-Sep	20.30	
9	5-Sep	19.25	
10	8-Sep	21.00	
11	9-Sep	21.35	
12	10-Sep	21.47	
13	11-Sep	20.83	
14	12-Sep	20.50	
15			
16	Hi Val		
17	Lo Val		
18	Av Val		
19	St Dev		

FIGURE 12.3

Task 4: Displaying the current date

1 Select cell E2 and enter the formula *=NOW()*

If a row of hash symbols (###) appears widen the column.

2 Format it to date format if necessary using the Format-Cells-Number command.

3 Enter the rest of the worksheet data.

4 Format the cell range B5 to B19 to two decimal places.

Task 5: Average and Standard Deviation

Rows 16 to 18 will contain respectively the maximum, minimum and average value of the shares over the two weeks. Row 19 will show the Standard Deviation – the extent to which share prices have fluctuated from the average.

1 In cell B16 enter the function *=MAX(B5:B14)*

2 In cell B17 enter the function *=MIN(B5:B14)*

3 Similarly apply the *Average* function to cell B18 and apply the *STDEV* function to cell B19.

Task 6: The IF function

We will now monitor whether the shares have shown an overall increase or decrease over the two weeks. We will use the logical function *IF()* so that if the share values increase then a 'share increase' message is displayed, if not a 'share decrease' message is displayed.

1 Activate cell D14 and enter the formula:
=IF(B14>B5,"share increase","share decrease")
A 'share increase' message should be displayed.

2 Test the function by amending the value of cell B14 to *14.50.* The message in cell D14 will change to 'share decrease' as the IF condition becomes false.

3 Use the **Edit-Undo** command to restore the original cell value.

Task 7: Date calculations

Dates can be added, subtracted and used in calculations. To make this point we will calculate the time in days between the opening and closing dates.

1 In cell D13 enter the label *Time in Days*.

2 In cell E13 enter the Formula *=A14-A5*

The result is 11 – the number of days. You may need to format the cell to a whole number – see section 2 above. The worksheet should now look like FIGURE 12.4.

	A	B	C	D	E
1		Share Analysis			
2					15/02/97 15:52
3	Date	Alpha			
4		Tours			
5	1-Sep	19.44			
6	2-Sep	19.44			
7	3-Sep	20.65			
8	4-Sep	20.30			
9	5-Sep	19.25			
10	8-Sep	21.00			
11	9-Sep	21.35			
12	10-Sep	21.47			
13	11-Sep	20.83		Time in Days	11
14	12-Sep	21.34		share increase	
15					
16	Hi Val	21.47			
17	Lo Val	19.25			
18	Av Val	20.51			
19	St Dev	0.86			
20					

FIGURE 12.4

3   Save the workbook as **SHARES.XLS**.

Task 8: Financial Functions

Now open Sheet2 of the workbook and try out the following financial functions:

1   **Future Value**. You are going to save £1000 a year at 10% interest for five years. Enter the following in a blank cell: *=FV(10%,5,-1000)*

The result is the value of your investment after five years – £6,105.10 (you may need to widen the column to show the result).

2   **Straight Line Depreciation.** You have bought a PC for £1000 and estimate that in four years it will be worth £300. We will use Paste Function.

First select a blank cell in the worksheet.

3   Open the **Insert** menu and select **Function.** The **Paste Function** dialog box appears.

4   Select **Financial** from the **Function Category** box and **SLN** from the **Function name** box – you may have to scroll down to find it.

5   Click the **OK** button. The second **Paste Function** dialog box appears.

6   Enter the arguments as shown in FIGURE 12.5.

Notice that as each box is selected Paste Function explains what you need to enter. It also tells you what the answer will be.

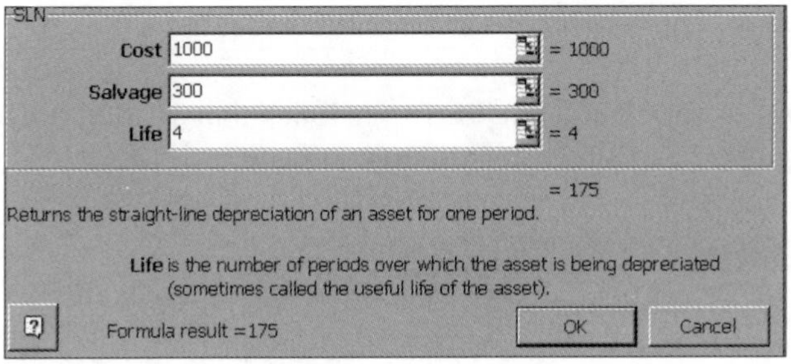

SLN

Cost 1000 = 1000

Salvage 300 = 300

Life 4 = 4

= 175

Returns the straight-line depreciation of an asset for one period.

Life is the number of periods over which the asset is being depreciated
(sometimes called the useful life of the asset).

Formula result =175

OK Cancel

FIGURE 12.5

7 Click the **OK** button on the dialog box.

The result is the annual amount of depreciation – £175.00.

8 Save and close the workbook.

Task 9: The Forecast function

The statistical functions Forecast and Trend allow you to predict future results based on past data. They are valuable tools in predicting many business trends including share prices, sales figures and stockholding needs.

1 Open the workbook **BOOKSLS** and make Sheet1 the active sheet. It records book sales and revenue for January to May.

2 First we will forecast June sales using the Forecast Function. However we must convert the months in column A to numbers in order for the function to work – see FIGURE 12.6. Make sure that you also enter the value for month 6.

	A	B	C	D	E	F
1			Book Sales - Current Year			
2						
3	Month	No. Sold	Revenue	Advertising	as % of Revenue	
4	1	850	2011	300	15%	
5	2	1010	3155	425	13%	
6	3	1175	3550	500	14%	
7	4	1430	4356	750	17%	
8	5	1710	5150	800	16%	
9	6					
10						

enter month 6

FIGURE 12.6

3 Select cell B9.

4 Open the **Insert** menu and select **Function** (or use the **Paste Function** button on the Standard Toolbar marked **fx** . The **Paste Function** dialog box appears.

5 Select **Statistical** from the **Function Category** box and **Forecast** from the **Function name** box – you may have to scroll down to find it.

157

6 Click the **OK** button. The second *Paste Function* dialog box appears.

7 Enter the arguments as shown in FIGURE 12.7. Notice that as each box is selected, Paste Function explains what you need to enter.

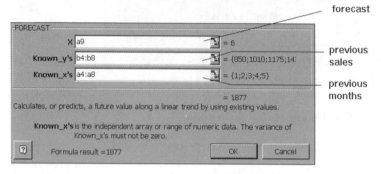

FIGURE 12.7

8 Finally click the **OK** button on the dialog box.

The result shows the sales forecast for month 6 – 1817 – based on a linear trend. The formula should be: *=FORECAST(A9,B4:B8,A4:A8)*

Task 10: The Trend function

Next we will find out how fast the cost of advertising will continue to rise, using the Trend function. We can use AutoFill to calculate it quickly. Use FIGURE 12.8 as a guide.

1 Highlight cell range D4 – D8.

2 Move the mouse pointer onto the AutoFill handle – the small square in the bottom right-hand corner of the selected cell range.

3 Hold down the *right* mouse button and drag down a few cells. Notice that the linear trend figures are shown for each cell as you do this.

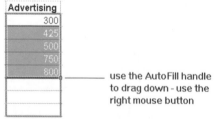

FIGURE 12.8

4 Release the mouse button. A menu appears.

5 Select either **Linear Trend** or **Growth Trend**. The trend for advertising expenditure is calculated.

6 Use **Edit-Undo** to undo the trend calculation if necessary.

7 Save and close the workbook.

Summary of commands

Menu commands show the menu name first, followed by the command to choose from the menu, e.g. **Edit-Clear** means open the **Edit** menu and select the **Clear** command.

Edit-Undo	Undo an operation
Format-Cells-Number	Format numeric data in cells
Insert-Function	Use Paste Function

Summary of Functions

■ Functions require you to supply information for their operations. These are called arguments. e.g. SUM(range) requires the argument cell range, to be added.

■ Arguments must be enclosed in brackets.

■ Optional arguments are shown in the lists that follow in square brackets – [ ]

■ These brackets are for your guidance only and should not be typed.

■ Function arguments are separated by commas. The commas must be typed.

HLOOKUP(x,range,index)
Look up a value in a table where the values are displayed horizontally.

VLOOKUP(x,range,index)
Look up values in a table where the values are displayed vertically.

x is the value that you want to look up; it can be entered as text, a number, or a cell reference.

Range is the range of cells forming the table.

Index tells you which column or row to look in.

FORECAST(x,known_y's,known_x's)
Predicts a future value based on existing values. The known values are existing x-values and y-values.

x is the data point whose value you are predicting.

Known_y's are the present range of values e.g. sales values.

Known_x's is the present intervals, e.g. days or months.

PMT(interest,term,principal,[,fv,type])
Gives the repayments required for a loan amount (principal) based on the interest rate and the term. Options are to enter future value and whether payment is made at the end of the period (type=0, the default) or at the beginning (type=1)

FV(interest,payments,amount[pv,type])

Gives the *Future Value* of an investment, based on a fixed interest rate, the number of payments and the amount of the payment. The payments are assumed to be equal throughout. Options are to enter present value (pv) and whether payment is made at the end of the period (type=0, the default) or at the beginning (type=1).

SLN(cost,salvage,life)

Calculates the depreciation of an asset using the *straight-line* method, based on the initial cost, its salvage value at the end of its life and the time period over which it is depreciated.

Information functions

COLUMNS(range)

Counts the number of columns in a specified range.

ISBLANK(value), ISNUMBER(value), ISTEXT(value).

IS functions check the type of value in a cell and report TRUE or FALSE accordingly, depending on whether the cell is blank, text etc.

Text Functions

EXACT(string1,string2)

Compares two text strings. Reports TRUE if they are the same or FALSE if they differ.

LEN(string)

Counts the number of characters in a text string.

Summary of unit

In this unit you have learned how to

- use the Lookup tables function

- display the current date

- use the Average and Standard Deviation functions

- use the IF function

- perform date calculations

- use the Forecast and Trend functions.

Creating and running macros

What you will learn in this unit

By the end of this unit you will be able to

- create and run a simple macro
- assign a macro to a button
- assign a macro to a toolbar
- test and delete a macro.

What you should know already

Skill	Covered in
How to start Excel	Unit 1
Basic mouse, menu and Windows operations	Unit 1
How to create a simple worksheet	Unit 2
How to use simple formulae and formatting	Units 1 – 3

What you need (optional)

To complete this unit you will need

- the workbook **INS_SLS** created in Unit 4
- the workbook **DISCOUNT** created in Unit 12
- the workbook **EUROSLS** created in Unit 5
- the workbook **DATABASE** created in Unit 8

Introduction

This unit introduces the last main element of Excel – macros. A macro lets you save a series of commands and run them again whenever one needs to use them. Nearly any series of keyboard strokes, menu choices and mouse movements can be stored in a macro and used again when required. There are several advantages to using macros.

- *Saving time* – issuing the same series of commands repeatedly is time consuming, a macro provides a short cut.
- *Reducing error* – long sequences of commands, mouse movements, and menu choices can be error prone. A macro achieves a consistent, correct result.

161

Excel 97 uses the Visual Basic programming language, an 'object oriented' programming language specially developed for Windows applications. In this unit we shall be creating some simple Visual Basic (VB) macros which automate simple tasks.

Hints and rules for macros

A macro is stored on a special module sheet.

Many macros can be stored on one module sheet.

Macros store commands using the Visual Basic (VB) programming Language.

Macros can control worksheets, charts and databases.

Every macro is saved and run under a different name. The macro name can be up to 255 characters long, must begin with a letter, and can consist of letters, numbers, full stops or underscores. Spaces are not allowed in macro names, so underscores or full stops are often used instead. Macro names are not case-sensitive.

A macro can be run in several ways, it can be assigned to a special button or menu choice. It can also be assigned a shortcut key – a single letter. Pressing down the *Ctrl* key and keying this letter will run the macro. The letter that you assign to a macro is case-sensitive, e.g. holding down the *Ctrl* key and pressing small *e* would run a particular macro; pressing *Ctrl* and capital *E* would not. This gives you a potential 52 shortcut key combinations. However, many are already used by Excel as keyboard shortcuts, e.g. *Ctrl-S* to save. Assigning the same key to a macro will override the keyboard shortcut while the workbook that contains the macro is open. If you use keyboard shortcuts it is best not to use these letters.

Task 1: Creating a simple macro

You can create a simple macro by using the macro recorder. Actions such as menu choices, mouse movements and keystrokes are then recorded and can be 'played back' when required. Our first macro will automate the simple task of adding the date and time to a worksheet. Instead of entering the NOW() function every time, you can use a shortcut by, say, pressing the *Ctrl* key and the letter *e*.

1 Open the workbook **DISCOUNT.XLS**. If you don't have this workbook then any workbook containing worksheet data will do, although you may need to adjust some of the cell references.

2 Select cell A1.

3 Open the Tools menu.

4 Choose Macro then Record New Macro.The Record Macro dialog box appears; use FIGURE 13.1.as a guide to completing it.

5 Enter the name **DATE_TIME** in the name box.

FIGURE 13.1

6 Enter the letter _e_ in the **Ctrl+** box. (Letters a – d are already used as Excel keyboard commands.)

7 Click the down arrow on the **Store macro in**: box.

8 Select the option **This Workbook.**

9 Select the **Description** box. It always contains the creation date plus the name of the author or organisation.

10 Add the description *Adds Current Date & Time*.

11 Click the **OK** button.

A single Stop Recording toolbar is displayed with a **Stop Macro** button on it – see FIGURE 13.2.

FIGURE 13.2

Task 2: Recording the macro

We are now ready to record the macro steps. All your actions are being recorded now, so don't issue any superfluous commands.

1 Enter the function *=NOW()* in cell A1.

2 Click the 'tick' button in the Formula Bar.

3 Open the **Format** menu.

4 Select **Cells** then the **Number** tab (even if already selected).

5 Select the **Date** category, then a suitable date/time format.

6 Click **OK** . The date appears, correctly formatted, in cell A1 of the **DISCOUNT** worksheet.

7 Click the **Stop Recording** button.

You have now recorded your first macro, **DATE_TIME**, which automates entering the date and time.

Troubleshooting – if your recording fails

The Excel Macro Recorder will record all your commands and key strokes – right or wrong. If you make a mistake while recording a simple macro then it is best to stop recording and proceed as follows.

- Open the Tools menu and select the Macro then the Macros option.
- Select the Macro from the dialog box.
- Click the **Delete** button.

Task 3: Running the macro using the shortcut key

1 Make sure that cell A1 is still selected.

2 Hold down the *Ctrl* key and press the *e* key. The macro will run, updating the date and time in cell A1.

Task 4: Running a macro by name

1 Open the Tools menu.

2 Select the Macro then the Macros option.

3 Select the macro **DATE_TIME** and click **Run**. The macro will run again.

Task 5: Macro viruses

1 Save and close the **DISCOUNT** workbook, then open it again. A dialog box will appear warning you of Macro viruses and giving you three options.

2 Click the **Tell me more** button.

You will see that a macro virus becomes active once the workbook(s) associated with the infected macro is opened. From then on, every workbook you open and save can be infected automatically with the macro virus. If other users on a network open infected workbooks, the macro virus can be passed on to their computers too. Also note that Excel 97 doesn't actually scan your disks for macro viruses – it merely displays a warning message whenever you try to open a workbook that uses macros. So to detect and remove viruses you would still need to have antivirus software installed.

3   Close the Help window and return to the dialog box.

The three options are:

Enable Macros i.e. open the workbook with the macros enabled – this is acceptable if the worksheet must use macros in order to work correctly and it comes from a reliable source. If you do not expect the workbook to contain macros, or you do not know or aren't certain about the reliability of its source, you might want to click –

Disable Macros i.e. open the workbook with macros disabled – this a safe option if you cannot rely on the source, e.g. the workbook is from an unfamiliar Internet site. However not only will you be unable to use essential macros, but other features may not work. You can still view, edit and save the macros but not run them.

Do not Open cancels the opening of the workbook.

If the virus message does not appear open the **Tools** menu and select **Options.**

When the dialog box appears select the **General** tab and check that the **Macro Virus Protection** option is selected.

4   Click the **Enable Macros** button.

Recap – the steps in running a macro

1 Activate the worksheet that the macro will control.

2 Open the **Tools** menu and select the **Macro-Record New Macro** options.

3 Complete the dialog box, e.g. name the macro and allocate the shortcut letter.

4 Record the actions in the macro.

5 Click the **Stop Macro** button.

Task 6: Creating a macro button

Earlier in this unit, we ran a macro in two ways: i) assigning it a shortcut key (*Ctrl-e*) and ii) running it from the macro menu. A third way is to assign a macro to a button. Clicking the button will run the macro, without needing to remember key strokes or menu choices. The button can either be part of the worksheet, or placed on a toolbar.

We will create a new macro **PRINT_IT** that will automate the printing of part of a worksheet.

1   Open the workbook **EUROSLS**.

If you don't have this workbook then any workbook containing worksheet data will do, although you may need to adjust some of the cell references.

We will create a print macro that prints the holiday sales held in cells A1 to F12 of the **Euro Hols Data** worksheet – make sure that this is the active sheet.

2 Open the **View** menu and select **Toolbars**.

3 Select **Forms** from the **Toolbars** list.

The Forms toolbar is displayed.

4 Click the **Create Button** tool – see FIGURE 13.3. The screen pointer changes to cross hairs.

FIGURE 13.3

5 Drag the screen pointer to draw a button that covers cells G2 and G3.

6 Let go of the mouse button. The button is drawn with the default name 'Button1'. We can reposition it later if necessary.

7 The **Assign Macro** dialog box opens automatically. Close the Forms toolbar.

8 Click the **Record** button on the dialog box.

The **Record Macro** dialog box appears.

9 Using FIGURE 13.4 as a guide, complete the dialog box as follows.

Enter the macro name as ***PRINT_HOLIDAYS***.

Leave the **Shortcut key** box blank – this macro will be run from a button.

Make sure that **This Workbook** is selected in the **Store Macro in** box (the cells to be printed will only apply to this workbook).

Complete the **Description** box as shown in FIGURE 13.4.

Click **OK**.

The macro is now assigned to the button and you are ready to start recording.

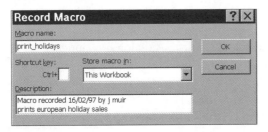

FIGURE 13.4

Task 7: Recording a printing macro

1 Make sure that your printer is turned on and connected.

2 Open the **File** menu and select **Page Setup**.

3 Click the **Sheet** tab.

4 Click the **Print Area** box.

5 Enter the cell references *A1:F12*

6 Click **OK** .

7 Open the **File** menu again and select **Print**. Choose 1 copy and whatever other settings you wish.

8 Click **OK** . Printing will now take place; when it is finished click the **Stop Recording** button. You have now created a print macro. In the next few tasks we will create a button that will run this macro and so print off the worksheet cells.

(!) **Troubleshooting** – see Task 11 below.

Task 8: Labelling the button

To change the size and colour of the button, or the text that appears on it, first you must select it.

1 Hold down the *Ctrl* key and click the button.

Selection handles appear round the button – see FIGURE 13.5

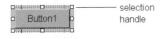

FIGURE 13.5

 If you forget to hold down the *Ctrl* key the macro will run.

2   Erase the default name.

3   Open the **Format** menu and select **Control**. A dialog box appears.

4   Choose 8 from the Size box.

5   Click the **down arrow** button on the **Colour** box.

6   Select a colour for the text.

7   Click OK. The button should be still selected.

8   Type the label on the button **Click to Print**.

9   Click elsewhere on the worksheet to deselect the button.

Task 9: Moving or sizing the button

1   Hold down the _Ctrl_ key and click the button. Selection handles appear.

2   To alter the size, hold down the _Ctrl_ key and drag one of the selection handles. See FIGURE 13.5 – the screen pointer will change to a double-headed arrow.

3   To move the button, place the screen pointer on the edge of the selected button – not on a selection handle – and drag. The button can now be moved.

Caution: Don't move the button within the print area or the button outline will be printed along with the worksheet.

4   Finally, press the _Esc_ key to de-select the button and remove the selection handles.

Task 10: Running the macro

1   If you are happy with the appearance of your button then try running it. Move the screen pointer on top of the button. The screen pointer becomes hand-shaped.

2   Click once, and the worksheet should print as before.

3   If you wish to cancel the printing, click the **Cancel** button.

Task 11: Viewing the macro

The macro has been recorded on a module sheet in the **EUROSLS** workbook.

1   Open the **Tools** menu.

2   Select the Macro then the Macros option. A dialog box appears.

3   Select the **PRINT_HOLIDAYS** macro.

4   Click the ▐Edit▐ button. The Module1 sheet appears.

5   ▐Maximise▐ it. It contains the macro in VB code. It is quite lengthy as all the standard page setup settings are listed.

6   Open the File menu and select the option 'Close and Return to Microsoft Excel'.

7   Save and close the **EUROSLS** workbook.

Troubleshooting – information only

 If a simple recorded macro doesn't work then it is usually easiest to delete it and re-record it.

Deleting a button

If you have made a mess of your button, or no longer need it, then you can delete it.

Select the button as before (*Ctrl-* click), then press the *Delete* key.

Deleting a macro

If the macro doesn't work correctly open the Tools menu and select the Macro, then the Macros options.

Select the macro name, then Delete from the dialog box.

Task 12: Consolidation

An unavoidable limitation of the **PRINT_HOLIDAY** macro that we have just created is that it only applies to one specific worksheet in the workbook **EUROSLS.XLS**. This is because it sets a print area that is unlikely to apply to any other worksheet, so each worksheet needs its own print macro.

1   Open the workbook **DATABASE**.

 If you don't have this workbook, any workbook containing worksheet data will do.

Using the previous operations in this unit as a guide, add a new macro to print off the **ORDERS** worksheet.

2   Call the macro **PRINT_ORDERS** and assign a shortcut key to it.

3   Create and assign a print button for this worksheet too.

4   Save and close the workbook.

Assigning a macro to a toolbar button

In previous tasks we learned three ways to run a macro

i) pressing shortcut keys, (*Ctrl* plus a letter)

ii) using the **Run** command from the **Macro** menu

iii) assigning it to a special button on the worksheet.

A fourth method is to attach a macro to a button on a toolbar. The macro can either take over the function of an existing button, or you can create a custom toolbar button. We will try the second method. We will add a button that will format a worksheet.

1   Open the workbook **INS_SLS**.

    If necessary drag aside the embedded chart to show the worksheet data.

    We are going to select a button, add it to the formatting toolbar, assign a macro to it and then record the macro.

 If you don't have this workbook then any workbook containing worksheet data will do, although you may need to adjust some of the cell references.

2   Open the **Tools** menu. Select **Customise**. A dialog box appears.

2   Click the **Commands** tab.

3   Select **Macros** from the **Categories** list – you may need to scroll down to see it.

4   Drag the custom button from the dialog box next to the **Bold** button on the Formatting Toolbar at the top of the window – see FIGURE 13.6. Do not close the dialog box.

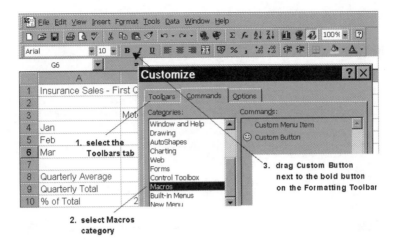

FIGURE 13.6

Task 14: Changing the toolbar button

1 Right click the **custom** button on the toolbar (not in the dialog box).

2 Select the option **Change Button Image** from the popup menu that appears.

3 Select a suitable icon. The custom button on the toolbar changes.

4 Now close the dialog box.

Task 15: Recording a formatting macro

1 Open the **Tools** menu. Select the **Macro** then the **Record New Macro** option.

A dialog box appears. Use FIGURE 13.7 as a guide to completing it.

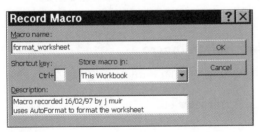

FIGURE 13.7

2 Type in the macro name **FORMAT_WORKSHEET**. Leave the Shortcut key entry blank.

3 Make sure that the **This Workbook** option is selected in the **Store macro in** section. (The formatting macro will only apply to this worksheet.)

4   Complete the description.

5   Click the **OK** button.

From now on your actions are being recorded.

6   Select the worksheet cells holding the data, i.e. cell range A1 to E10.

7   Open the **Format** menu and select **AutoFormat**.

8   Select the format **Colorful 2** from the **AutoFormat** box.

9   Click **OK**.

10   Click the **Stop Macro** button.

Task 16: Assigning the macro

1   Open the **Tools** menu. Select **Customise**. A dialog box appears.

2   Right click the **custom** button on the toolbar.

3   Select the option **Assign Macro** from the popup menu that appears.

A dialog box appears.

4   Select the macro **FORMAT_WORKSHEET** from the dialog box.

5   Click **OK**.

6   Close the **Customise** dialog box.

Task 17: Testing the toolbar button macro

First we will restore the worksheet to its normal format.

1   Make sure that the cell range is still selected.

2   Open the **Format** menu and select **AutoFormat** again.

3   Select the format **None** from the list box – you may have to scroll down to see it.

4   Click **OK**.

The worksheet is now restored to its previous format.

5 Now click the special custom button that you have created on the Formatting Toolbar. The macro reformats the worksheet to the format previously recorded.

 If a simple recorded macro doesn't work then it is usually easiest to delete it and re-record it – see Task 11.

Task 18: Deleting a Custom Toolbar button

1 Open the **Tools** menu. Select **Customise**. A dialog box appears.

2 Click the **Commands** tab.

3 Drag the custom button from the toolbar back to the dialog box.

4 Close the workbook **INS_SLS**. If you don't wish to keep the formatting or the macro then don't save it.

Summary of commands

Menu commands show the menu name first, followed by the command to choose from the menu, e.g. **Edit-Clear** means open the **Edit** menu and select the **Clear** command.

Ctrl-[letter]	Run macro using shortcut key
Ctrl-[select]	Select screen button
File-Page Setup	Modify page settings
Format-AutoFormat	Select automatic worksheet format
Format-Cells-Number	Format a date or number
Format-Control	Format a selected object, e.g. button
Tools-Customise-Commands	Add/remove custom toolbar button
Tools-Macro-Macros	Run, edit or delete a macro
Tools-Macro-Record New Macro	Record a new macro
Tools Options-General	Display/hide virus warning messages
View-Toolbars-Forms	Display/hide Forms toolbar

Summary of unit

In this unit you have learned how to

- create a simple macro
- record a macro
- run a macro using a shortcut key
- run a macro by name
- enable and disable macros
- assign a macro to a button
- create a print macro
- label a button
- move or size a button
- view a macro
- assign a macro to a toolbar
- test a macro
- delete a Custom Toolbar button
- delete a macro.

	G	H	I	J	K
NCES - TERM 1					
	Week 6	Week 7	Week 8	Week 9	Week 10
	£ 495.00	£ 365.00	£ 235.00	£ 105.00	-£ 25.00
	£ 495.00	£ 365.00	£ 235.00	£ 105.00	-£ 25.00
	£ 60.00	£ 60.00	£ 60.00	£ 60.00	£ 60.00
	£ 35.00	£ 35.00	£ 35.00	£ 35.00	£ 35.00
	£ 15.00	£ 15.00	£ 15.00	£ 15.00	£ 15.00
	£ 20.00	£ 20.00	£ 20.00	£ 20.00	£ 20.00
	£ 130.00	£ 130.00	£ 130.00	£ 130.00	£ 130.00
	£ 365.00	£ 235.00	£ 105.00	-£ 25.00	-£ 155.00

	A	E	F	G	H	I	J	K
1		PERSONAL FINANCES - TERM 1						
2								
3	INCOME	Week 4	Week 5	Week 6	Week 7	Week 8	Week 9	Week 10
7	Part Time Job				£ 20.00	£ 20.00	£ 20.00	£ 20.00
8	Parents					£ 30.00		
9	Total Income	£ 750.00	£ 615.00	£ 480.00	£ 385.00	£ 320.00	£ 225.00	£ 130.00
10								
11	EXPENDITURE							
12	Accommodation	£ 65.00	£ 65.00	£ 65.00	£ 65.00	£ 65.00	£ 65.00	£ 65.00
13	Food and Travel	£ 35.00	£ 35.00	£ 30.00	£ 30.00	£ 30.00	£ 30.00	£ 30.00
14	Books	£ 15.00	£ 15.00	£ -	£ -	£ -	£ -	£ -
15	Other	£ 20.00	£ 20.00	£ 20.00	£ 20.00	£ 20.00	£ 20.00	£ 30.00
16	Total Expenditure	£ 135.00	£ 135.00	£ 115.00	£ 115.00	£ 115.00	£ 115.00	£ 125.00
17								
18	CLOSING BALS.	£ 615.00	£ 480.00	£ 365.00	£ 270.00	£ 205.00	£ 110.00	£ 5.00

	A	B	C	D	E	F
1	Insurance Sales - First Quarter					
2						
3		Motor	Life	Property	Total	
4	Jan	1465	1243	2456	5164	
5	Feb	1345	1456	1987	4788	
6	Mar	1132	2310	1598	5040	
7						
8	Quarterly Average	1314	1670	2014	4997	
9	Quarterly Total	3942	5009	6041	14992	
10	% of Total	26.29%	33.41%	40.29%		
11						
12		This worksheet shows a sales analysis of				
13		the three major insurance categories				
14						
15						

	A	B	C	D	E
1	Order No.	Order Date	Co.Ref	Co. Name	Value
2	14005	11-Mar	955	Tilley Transport	1678.00
3	14003	11-Mar	1289	Marsden Products	4456.00
4	14009	12-Mar	1289	Marsden Products	1652.54
5	14007	09-Mar	1453	Wilson Garages	2654.00
6	14000	10-Mar	1453	Wilson Garages	3200.00
7	14002	11-Mar	1453	Wilson Garages	98.76
8	14008	12-Mar	2245	Goldfield Stables	123.85
9	14006	10-Mar	2375	Patel Kitchens	55.54
10	14001	08-Mar	2413	Patel Industries	1466.00
11	14004	10-Mar	2413	Patel Industries	567.00
12					

Appendix 5

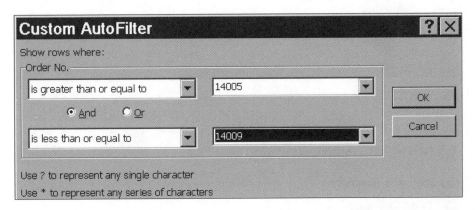

Appendix 6

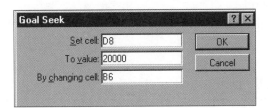

Appendix 7

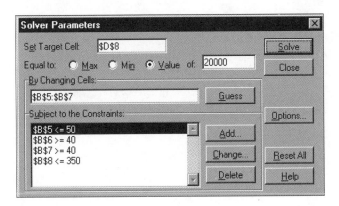

Appendix 8

1a. IPMT funtion.

1b. RATE function.

2a   ROUNDUP or ROUNDDOWN functions.

2b. SUBTOTAL function.

3a. COUNTBLANK function.

3b. NORMDIST function.

4a. REPLACE function.

4b. TRIM function.

4c   UPPER or LOWER functions.

5a. TYPE function.

5b. ISBLANK or ISERR/ISERROR functions.

Glossary

Active Cell	The cell currently selected and shown by a heavy border. In Excel 97, a cell can contain up to 32,000 characters
Address	Consists of two coordinates – the column letter followed by the row number (as in a street map)
AutoFormat feature	Allows you to format your worksheets automatically, offering 17 built-in formats to choose from; Excel will automatically detect which worksheet areas should be headings, data, totals etc.
AutoSum button	Offers the quickest way of adding a column of figures. It is on the Standard toolbar and is marked with the Greek letter sigma (Σ),
Box or cell	Where a column and a row intersect.
Cell reference	Consists of two coordinates – the column letter followed by the row number (as in a street map).
ChartWizard	Allows you to create simple charts using four steps (see Unit 3); allows you to change the chart type and other parameters.
Close button (an 'X')	This closes either Excel or one of the workbooks. If you click one of these buttons by mistake you will need to open Excel and/or your workbook(s) again.
Column and Row headings	These contain the column references (letters) and the row references (numbers). Jointly they give the cell reference or address, e.g. A1, D5.
Command bar	In Excel 97, the common term for a toolbar and a menu.
Control Menu boxes	These offer commands such as resizing and closing the window.
Cutting and pasting	Cutting cells physically removes them from their original location so that they can be pasted to a new one. This is a similar operation to copying.
Doughnut chart	This is like a pie chart; it shows the relative contribution of various quantities to a total. However, unlike a pie chart it is not restricted to one data series.
Drawing Toolbar	This allows you to draw a variety of shapes on your worksheet – circles, rectangles, arrows etc. It also allows you to add colour and text effects.
Formula Bar	This shows whatever is entered in the active cell.
Formulae	These tell the spreadsheet to perform calculations, e.g. add the values in a column or work out a percentage.

179

Goal Seek tool	Can substitute various values for a variable in a formula; it cannot determine what the 'best' ones are for your purpose.
Macro	Lets you save commands in a special macro sheet. The commands can then be run automatically whenever one needs to use them. Nearly any series of keystrokes, menu choices and mouse movements can be stored in a macro and used again when required.
Maximize button (a square)	This either increases the size of the Excel application window to fill the screen or increases the size of the document window so that it fills the whole of the application window.
Minimize button (a line)	This either reduces Excel to a button on the Taskbar or the document window to a small icon within the application window.
Office Assistant	New to Excel 97, this supplements other Help features by answering questions typed in ordinary English.
Paste Link command	Ensures that when the original workbook changes the copy changes also.
Reference Area	This shows the row and column number of the active cell.
Restore button (overlapping squares)	This restores an individual window to its original size.
Sheet names	Each sheet is marked with a name tab – the name in bold indicates which sheet is currently selected or 'active'.
Solver	This can solve certain types of problem. It will juggle with multiple values for variables and find the combination producing the optimum or target result, e.g. it can determine the most profitable mix of products, schedule staff to minimise the wages till, or allocate working capital to its most profitable use.
Spreadsheet	This is a grid of vertical columns and horizontal rows.
Status Bar	Displays information about the current command.
Trendline	Useful for emphasising relationships between different data series.
'What's This?' feature	Offers 'context-sensitive' tips, i.e. tips specific to the Excel feature that you are currently using.

Index

Index

Cell contents

Tools-options - view - formulas

Average

click on cells f^x - statistical - average
highlight area

File extensions

Click on view options

Auto Calculation

tools- options - calculations

Bodmas

Formulas

= Average (A1: A10)

= sum (--:--) or high area to be added

Absolute Ref

eg B3* $B$7

Scientific Notation
place decimal to right of 1st figure, then number
of figures decimal place, then E + how many places
point has moved
eg 3,125,689,480 = 3.125E+9